Advance Praise

*No one more than Glenn Edwards exemplifies how charac-
ter—being positive, truly caring about the people around you,
always keeping your word and doing what is right—leads
to accomplishment. It is not an accident that every venture
Glenn touches finds success, because his character, optimism,
and energy bring out the best in everyone around him. Glenn's
story teaches fundamental lessons to all who seek the secrets
of true success in business, and in life.*

—RICHARD ALBERT, PARTNER AT MORVILLO
ABRAMOWITZ GRAND IASON & ANELLO PC

*My father is as comfortable entertaining a prime minister as
he is speaking with a cab driver. I have been elbow to elbow
with him as he negotiated with the CEO of a Fortune 500
company, and I witnessed him inspire hundreds of my friends
through his blog when there seemed like there was no hope*

during the Great Recession. What it all boils down to is my father loves business and loves to live his life. Although he never read the Stoics, he is a stoic philosopher. Although he never attended business school, he is a student of business. I am lucky to have my Father as a mentor and coach. When he shared his simple philosophy through his blog, he had no idea it would inspire so many. Thank you, Dad, for having the courage to turn your blog into a book.

—JORDAN EDWARDS, PRESIDENT AT
MIXOLOGY CLOTHING COMPANY

I have had the pleasure of interacting with Glenn Edwards on both a professional and personal level. As his accountant and advisor, I have worked with Glenn on many successful business ventures, and his business acumen is second to none. One of Glenn's most admirable qualities is his loyalty to his family, friends, and business associates. I am honored to call Glenn Edwards my friend.

—STEVEN MADONNA, CPA AT MADONNA & COMPANY, LLP

We are humbled to be considered in honoring our dear friend and mentor Glenn. One of the greatest gifts we can give to others is inspiration to truly believe in our dreams. True prosperity is the result of well-placed intentions and confidence in ourselves and others while offering a significant contribution to the world with our presence. Glenn's very being exemplifies the truest essence of these words. At the soul of our incredible business opportunity, experience, connection, and friendship with Glenn, there is an unspoken knowing of faith, trust, and goodness in each other and in humanity. We are humbled and honored to be mentored by Glenn. As a brilliant thought leader and visionary, Glenn's unwavering inspiration, words, and wisdom have lent us confidence as we navigate uncharted territories in developing a women-operated retail district and destination in downtown Springfield, Massachusetts. With his leadership, and gentle nudges, we are making a significant contribution to the retail renaissance, as we breathe life into the once vacant and now very vibrant, beautiful, and profitable space known as The Shops at Marketplace. The opportunities and experiences that are being cocreated and offered—such as incubating new businesses and gifting the space for community events and experiences at the shops— would not be possible without Glenn's kindness, vision, wisdom, and generous spirit. Glenn often reminds us of being mindful and aware of the givers and takers of the world. Glenn is a giver. We are incredibly humbled by and grateful for his generosity, wisdom, and experience of life. Glenn Edwards is a rare and wonderful human being, and we are blessed to call this amazing man our dear friend and mentor.

—MIKKI LESSARD AND NANCY FETH, FOUNDERS
OF SIMPLY GRACE & SIMPLY SERENDIPITY,
THE SHOPS AT MARKETPLACE

Coming Into Your Own

Glenn Edwards

Coming

Into

Your

Own

How to Develop the Morals and Mindset
of a (Future) Business Leader

LIONCREST
PUBLISHING

COMING INTO YOUR OWN
How to Develop the Morals and Mindset
of a (Future) Business Leader

ISBN   978-1-61961-649-3 *Paperback*
       978-1-61961-650-9 *Ebook*

This book is dedicated to my children.

May the lessons I have learned be passed along to future generations.

Contents

. . . . .

Acknowledgments

• • • • •

Let me be honest here; before you ever read the first page, I should acknowledge my son, Jordan. Without his insistence, I never would have undertaken this journey to write a book. He has completely bought into a theme you will read here—the importance of tenacity—because that is what it took for him to get me to put my thoughts, beliefs, and theories on life and business into words. When Jordan was old enough to understand, the first of our thousands of conversations began on a drive to Vermont, and they continued on the drives to either Hebrew school or soccer games. Years later, Jordan felt that all my life's "Glennisms," as he calls them, were important to convey to others. Thank you so much for being a great son, partner, and instigator for writing this book. I hope you enjoy it as much as you loved *Kemo Sabe Wisdom* by Tom Yoder (inside joke).

One of the most thrilling parts of writing this book is giving credit to my parents. Every day, my father showed my brothers and me that hard work and honesty weren't options; they were everything. I have never met a person who had a bad word to say about Irving Edwards. Though he's eighty-nine years old and long since retired, people still remember him and praise him for their time together. I worked with and learned from him for twenty-five years and never regretted it. I continue to learn from him to this day.

I acknowledge my mother too. "Grandma Norma" for many years to everyone she met, she taught us to treat employees like customers. She knew that employers and employees were interdependent and neither could be successful without the other. I miss her so much, but I am so lucky to have the memories and the lessons she taught me.

Instead of just acknowledging Book in a Box, my publisher, I will give them a reference: *Use them if you want to write a book!* Thanks to Kathleen, Kevin, and Chas. You made writing and speaking about my life an enjoyable experience. Even with my bad ADD, you kept me on topic and never got frustrated with me. Without your guidance, this never would have been completed (on time).

As you read this book, you will see mentioned a few highly admired friends who also contributed: Sam, Brad, Joe, Rabbi New, Chris, and Steve. Your sincere and thoughtful contributions are vital to this book. In different ways, I love how each of you conducts yourself in business and life. You represent the many people who have impacted my life.

Lastly, I save my greatest appreciation for my wife. Lisa copes with me and has been my rock through the best of times—and more importantly, through the worst. Lisa is one of the strongest people I know. Everyone needs someone like her in their corner to make the most of every opportunity. No matter how it turns out, I get to come home to her. I love her for all she has done for me, my career, and our family.

Introduction

· · · · ·

How many times do we say we can't do something, without even trying?

My wife, Lisa, is a tremendous dancer and choreographer. In college, she thrived in this role, designing a variety of showstopping numbers and helping the local talent shine.

Every now and then, a routine would require her to perform onstage with her troupe, but for the most part, she sat back in the wings and watched her dancers masterfully execute their routines. She was happy in this role, reveling in her dancers' success.

One day, however, a particularly involving routine forced her to step out of her comfort zone and participate—not as a dancer, but as a singer.

Lisa wasn't a bad singer. She could certainly get through a song without embarrassing herself, but singing in front of a live audience didn't exactly fill her heart with anticipation. Of course, as they say in the theater, the show must go on. In a few weeks, she had to face her fears and deliver a tune.

Fortunately, she had a wonderful mentor, a professor at her school who was convinced that he could teach her to sing. She hesitated at first, but he wouldn't take no for an answer. For those few weeks, she was his pupil to mold. When it came time for her number, she pulled it off without a hitch, no doubt learning a thing or two about herself in the process.

I love telling this story for several reasons, not the least of which is that it speaks to my wife's tireless dedication to her craft. She could have said no. She could have said singing made her uncomfortable, and she preferred someone else to do it. Instead, she committed to the job, set realistic goals, and succeeded with flying colors.

This lesson helped her overcome her fear during some difficult jobs early in her career, and later during some difficult choices involving our family and her design career. In fact, you could even say that it led to a better outcome for all the tough decisions she has made in life.

EVERYONE CAN USE A GOOD MENTOR

A lot of people think they're only good at one thing. I find this especially common in young people, who often don't fully appreciate what they're capable of. So much of this is mentality: if you think you can't do something, then you're probably right. However, if you depend on yourself and make the effort to get better, you can do anything.

Lisa's story also highlights the importance of mentorship. Whenever I can, I tell people to find someone else whose talent, skills, and integrity reflect the person they want to become. Obviously, you never want to lose your own identity, but you do want to find someone who will help you become the best possible version of yourself and teach you some new tricks along the way.

That said, be careful whom you latch onto. Avoid the people who take shortcuts, who operate in a moral gray area. Especially in business, a lot of people will say that the ends justify the means, but I don't believe that. To me, there's only one way to get through life: the right way.

As we move through our careers, sometimes we're the student, and sometimes we're the teacher. During the same production that called her to sing, Lisa mentored an Army vet named Keith who had recently returned to school. He was already a phenomenal singer, but my wife saw the makings of a great dancer as well. She worked tirelessly with him during that production, and later he went on to have a successful dancing career.

When you believe in your abilities, whether they're already refined or still need a little polish, you can throw yourself into any situation without reservation.

We have worked to instill this value in our children as well, sometimes quite literally. When my son, Jordan, was about six months old, I threw him into our pool so that he would learn to swim, and I like to say that I have never stopped throwing any of my children into the pool since.

Some people freak out when I say this, thinking that I put too much pressure and responsibility on my kids at too young an age. However, I've found that the more responsibility I give to talented, hardworking people, the more they thrive. They don't flail about and try to get out of the water. Instead, they learn to swim.

I can think of no better core value for young professionals: learn to swim. Have faith that you will not only survive, but also thrive. When you find something you can't do yet, find someone else to show you a path forward.

Now that he's grown and in charge of two businesses, Jordan reflects these values and makes them his own every day. At thirty-one, he's already a tireless worker for our company. He's often the first to arrive and the last to get home. Somehow, he has still found the time to keep up his martial-arts practice, read an endless number of books, and meet the woman of his dreams.

Recently, our company bought some new property in Brownsville, Texas. For the first time, Jordan took the lead 100 percent. He organized all the financing, put the book together, and found the right outfit for the purchase. Watching him come into his own like this, I couldn't have been more proud. Once again I had thrown him into the pool, and once again he took off swimming.

In both my wife and my son, I see the core elements of leadership: hard work, integrity, and positivity. Know who you want to be, where you want to learn, and whom you want to learn from. Then, set out to answer those questions, seeking trusted mentors as needed along the way. When you truly commit to success, nobody can stop you from getting there.

ANYONE CAN LEARN TO LEAD

This is a book about coming into your own, about

becoming the leader you want to be rather than the one you think others want you to be.

For my Lisa and me, the wonderful thing about watching our children grow is seeing how they've taken their parents' best attributes—my wife's creativity and my hard-driving business approach—and forge paths for themselves that are entirely their own. This philosophy embodies the core theme of this book. It's not about being like me. Rather, it's about applying some tried-and-true practices to your own life and circumstances, so that you can be the best version of yourself.

As a leader and a mentor, your job is to oversee everyone on your team and make sure they're performing to the best of their abilities. First, you must identify your talent. Who are your A, B, and C players, and who is ready to take on more responsibility? Second, extract talent from all your players. Often, it will be talent they didn't even know they had. Third, have confidence in yourself and in your team to get the job done. Don't walk away from your challenges. Invest in them, and work to get the most you can out of the experience.

In my own career, people have often said, "Glenn, your greatest fault in business is you never fire anybody." Maybe this is indeed a weakness, but I've felt it was my greatest strength. In my experience, every company has a place for its A, B, and C players. Good leaders know how each player fits in and how each person can best be utilized.

Naturally, everyone sets their own limitations and personal expectations. C-level players are happy just to show up to work, do their job, and go home to their families. I may want more for some of them, but if they're satisfied, then I should respect that.

B players often have the drive, but many haven't quite learned how to access all the tools at their disposal. If they have the ability, interest, and work ethic to elevate their games, however, they can become B+ or even A players. Sometimes they do, and sometimes they don't. In mentoring them, I try to do the right things for the right reasons and motivations and help them find their way.

The A players you can spot a mile away. They don't have to be great at everything, though. For instance, I wouldn't call myself the smartest guy around, and I certainly wasn't the best student. However, I was an incredible salesman, had a strong work ethic, and infused my work with integrity, honesty, and a people-first attitude. This combination has driven my A-level success, despite whatever shortcomings others might have seen.

You never want to see your A players rest on their laurels. After all, talent and ability are nothing if they're not put to good use. Let the rest of your team drive them. Not everybody is Lebron James, but even Lebron needs the B and C players around him to become a champion. Some of those players may spend more time on the bench than on the court, but they still contribute to team harmony in a multitude of ways.

Whenever I share this concept, I think of Marge, a receptionist at one of my former companies. Marge was already in her eighties by the time I met her, but she made herself invaluable. Marge made everybody smile as they walked in, happily directing visitors and callers to the right person and cementing a positive work environment for everyone. She didn't lead, but she didn't need to in order to leave her mark.

WHAT IT TAKES TO LEAD

My other son, Tyler, likes to make his own way. Whether in high school, college, or his first job, we didn't always know what he was working on, but we trusted that he would come out ahead.

Tyler trusts his instincts to make the right decisions, and those instincts rarely let him down. Only twenty-five, in three years he's risen from an entry-level analyst to director of acquisitions. In fact, he recently completed his first deal for the company, bringing in a tremendous asset in the process.

I'm proud of Tyler. He has the self-confidence to do everything on his own, all while maintaining strong relationships with his family and friends too. Often, especially when we're young, we don't think we're capable of much, and thus, we never push ourselves as hard as we should.

Tyler's girlfriend, Jessica, was much like this. In my many conversations with her during the first few years of her career, I saw the raw talent of a young professional-to-be—talent that she did not yet know she had. Where in her first job she was subjected to horrible bosses who killed her self-esteem, through personal growth and hard work, she is now an account executive at Snapchat. Where once she was timid and afraid to take on any new responsibilities, today she's writing millions of dollars' worth of business for a rapidly growing social-media company. Today, you can't hold her back. All traces of the insecure young woman I first met are gone. I can't wait to see where her career takes her next.

The point is, when a young person says to me that they can't amount to anything or they don't have what it takes,

I think of these two people. Some see the path before them right away, while others need a little mentoring and encouragement to get there. At any rate, the point is that anyone can get there.

Frankly, some need to fail a little bit before they can learn to take control of their professional lives. It's not an easy path to walk, but with the proper support, it can be a productive one.

Ultimately, it comes down to one question: how do you know whether you have what it takes if you don't know what it takes in the first place? This is the value of mentorship, and it's the question I hope to answer in this book. Find someone to push you forward and show you what you can become, so you can learn not only what you truly want, but also how to achieve it.

WHO IS THIS BOOK FOR?

Between 2007 and 2010, it felt as if the whole world was collapsing. The economy tanked and unemployment skyrocketed, and the recovery afterward was middling at best. During this time, I watched as two of my three children emerged from college and into a job market that either wouldn't hire them or wouldn't pay them what they were worth.

Fortunately, my own businesses had proven somewhat recession-resistant. The growth I had enjoyed the previous four years may have slowed to a crawl, but on the stormy seas of commerce, I could hold on to the rails of my little ship and maintain my course.

This relative stability allowed me to observe what was going on around me. Through my kids, I saw an entire Millennial workforce that felt helpless, forgotten even, amid such economic uncertainty. In my own small way, I wanted to do something about it. After giving it some thought, I decided to blog.

More than anything, I wanted to be a voice of encouragement. Perhaps through my own life experiences and my professional ups and downs, I could offer guidance to a generation that sorely needed it.

The blog caught on. People of all ages read it and engaged in what I had to say. As time went on, our economy recovered—and so did the careers of many people who contributed to our discussions. Eventually, as my own children and their peers found their way, I stopped writing, happy with whatever contribution I'd made to others' success.

My blog lay dormant for years, until Jordan rediscovered it about a year ago. A voracious reader always looking for the next bit of leadership advice, Jordan saw the blog in a new light. He was convinced my message would resonate with other young leaders like him. I wasn't so sure, but Jordan's tireless advocacy won out, and here we are.

With this book, I hope to continue the conversation my blog began. Mostly, I want to help those who are starting out, the active young minds who are thinking a few years ahead and setting ambitious goals for themselves. However, I also want to help seasoned professionals like myself hone their mentorship skills and help future generations of business leaders hit the ground running.

In life, we are often mentors in one area and students in another. This book speaks to both the mentor and the student in each of us.

THE CORE PRINCIPLES OF LEADERSHIP

To me, leadership isn't just about getting results, but about earning respect. Successful leaders lift up the people they work with. They help others become better than they ever could have been on their own. They make it a joy to go to work, not a chore. They respect both the nature of their work and the people they work with. Most importantly, just as they support others, good leaders know others support them.

To show you how to become the kind of leader who is both effective and respected, this book explores the following seven themes:

1. Mentality: Have a positive attitude every day. You can achieve great things when you wake up every day believing in yourself. Building a positive mindset takes practice and persistence. Anyone can do it.

2. Values: Commit to honesty and integrity. Treat people better than you would treat yourself, and always make sure to leave them smiling.

3. Strategy: Know what you want to do, before you must do it. Understand your competition. Understand your product better than anybody else, and make sure you put the right team together to implement your strategy.

4. Discipline: Get up earlier, work harder, and train, train, train.

5. Competition and collaboration: Don't fear your competition. Embrace them. Know what they're all about. Identify where you can differentiate yourself.

6. Resilience: You get beat up in business. If you don't think you're going to get beat up, don't go to work. Keep reasonable expectations, and seek balance between the natural highs and lows of your job.

7. Charitable motivations: Whatever role you play, find a way to give back. Be sincere. Don't give because

it fulfills a requirement. Identify a cause you're passionate about, and find a way to help.

The following chapters are designed to help you develop the morals and mindset of a future business leader. Through these strategies, my hope is you will become, not just a better, more compassionate professional, but a better person as well.

HOW I CAME TO WRITE THIS BOOK

I owe so much of my perspective to my parents, who were the most ethical, honest, hardworking people I've ever known. As part of the Greatest Generation, the group of Americans who came into their own during the Great Depression and World War II, they rose through the middle class to grow a family and a business based on hard work and integrity. They forged these values in me, and I have worked hard to share them with my own children.

I never saw my father in the morning. He was already off to work by the time I woke up, and he usually didn't get home until dinner. To me, he exemplified what a good, honest businessman was supposed to be.

With my first paper route at the age of six, I applied my father's example to my own life. The work wasn't glamorous, and I only brought in a penny a paper, but I wanted to distinguish myself as one of those neighborhood kids who always had a job. By ten, I owned my own newspaper route. By fourteen, I had three or four other kids delivering papers for me.

I've always worked. I've always made money. I've always given back to my customers and my employees. I like to say nothing in my career has changed. I just don't deliver newspapers anymore.

To me, "work ethic" is a criminally underrated term. Sure, a lot of people think they have it, but too many wouldn't recognize a good work ethic if it was staring them in the face.

To develop a strong work ethic, you must know someone who has one. You have to identify someone you admire and say, "I want to do that. That's who I want to be." For me, it was my father, but it can be anyone you admire.

The experiences of professional athletes, from the best to the worst of them, often exemplify the application of work ethic. To break into the professional ranks, they must work harder and perform better than everyone else around them. Because so few make careers as professional athletes, they have zero margin for error.

If you are lucky enough to go pro, you can't rest on your laurels. You must keep that work ethic up, all while learning to elevate your game. Becoming a pro isn't an end, but a new beginning.

That's the kind of mentality it takes to succeed. Don't rest on your laurels. Once you've achieved one goal, set another one and continue to grow. Take pride in what you've accomplished and seek joy along the way, but strive to be something more too.

A ROAD MAP FOR THE JOURNEY AHEAD

Think of this book as one possible road map for your future. I've seen the power of these strategies firsthand, and I know they work. However, if you read something and disagree, hopefully you'll still learn something about yourself in the process. Either way, I'm confident this book can help you expand your own concepts of leadership.

I've had a fun, interesting career. I've had my ups and downs, but I like to say I've always been up, even when things were down. I see opportunity in everything, and I think everyone can benefit from such a mindset. Not everything has to go your way for you to know which way you want to go.

The chapters in this book will share not only my own experiences, but those of my trusted friends, family members, or colleagues to illustrate my points and add diversity to the discussion.

Each of these people has impacted my life tremendously, and my admiration for them has no boundaries. Success didn't come easily for any of them. Yet through their hard work, honesty, and integrity, they all became leaders in their fields.

One such contributor is Brad Weisbord, one of the shrewdest people I've ever met. In fact, at only thirty years old, Brad is a premier horse owner.

Brad isn't successful just because he's smart, but because he knows how to turn a perceived disadvantage into an opportunity. When he was young, Brad loved to play lacrosse. Coaches were reluctant to let him play, because he was a bit undersized, but after he learned to use his skills to his advantage, they couldn't keep him off the field.

In life, we often find ourselves trying to play someone else's game instead of our own. Brad couldn't outmatch his opponents through his reach or his height, but he didn't have to. Instead, he played below his opponents. When they played high, he played low. He brought them down to his level, masterfully swerving underneath and around the other players, before they knew what happened.

That's what I believe works in business: take what you have, and use it to your advantage. If you're shrewd, use that. If you're quick, use that. If you're tall, use that. Use everything to your advantage. Don't let it hold you back. Turn your negatives into positives. Accentuate your attributes. Make your supposed deficits work for you.

LEADERSHIP BEGINS WITH A POSITIVE MINDSET

As we get ready to launch into the first chapter, I'll leave you with one last story. When I was seventeen or eighteen, I got my driver's license. Soon after, my father bought me a suit and told me to drop a handful of fliers off at two or three local hospitals to see if we could drum up some business. Despite my best efforts, one of the hospitals wouldn't let me in to speak with them. They had been using the same two agencies for a hundred years, they said, and they saw no reason to give their business over to some kid in a suit.

I could have given up without my father thinking any worse of me. Instead, I kept after them for five years. I used sticky notes to keep track of leads back then, and every three months, the note marked "Long Beach Hospital" rotated back through. As soon as it did, I headed back down there to remind them who I was and see if their circumstances had changed.

Finally, a year out of college, I got my first order from them. Ten years later, I was on their board of trustees, organizing golf outings and other public events for them.

Every time I meet someone ready to set out on their own career, I tell this story. Some have asked if I wasted five years, if I could have been more productive cultivating other leads during this time instead. To these people, I say it wasn't about gaining a customer, but rather about gaining a customer for life. No matter how many times they said no, I resolved to visit that hospital every three months until they said yes. Giving up wasn't an option.

For me, this experience set a standard for the rest of my life. Set your eyes on what you want, and don't stop until you get it. Through it all, though, remember to keep a positive mindset.

CHAPTER ONE

The Power of a Positive Mindset

• • • • •

I like sports analogies, because it's often easier to see people overcome monumental obstacles on the field than it is in the office. In that regard, the 2017 Rose Bowl made for one heck of a story.

The game was a classic back-and-forth between two very talented teams, USC and Penn State, with the former ultimately coming out on top, 52–49. Truthfully, it was anyone's game up until the final moments, when USC pulled out ahead for good in one of the highest-scoring games in Rose Bowl history.

I saw so many chances for failure throughout the contest, so many chances to panic and run away. Yet these young players kept their heads in the game, ready to rise to the next challenge. Like everyone else watching, I was riveted from kickoff to USC's final drive as the clock wound down.

When I watch games like this, I think of the kids living it. Especially in college football, so much is on the line. For many, their entire careers hang in the balance. It's high drama on a big stage, and the best of them absolutely live for it.

In the Rose Bowl, no star shined brighter than USC's nineteen-year-old freshman quarterback, Sam Darnold, one of the youngest players on the field that day. No doubt he gave the performance of the year, but his team, his coaches, and the crowd also rewarded his every effort. Only time will tell if that was the greatest day of Darnold's athletic life, or if he simply set a new standard for a future that is now wide open for him.

Either way, I was fascinated by his poise and maturity during the postgame interview. I'm sure the reporter expected him to behave like a normal nineteen-year-old and gush about his performance and the experience he just had. To my great surprise, he showed tremendous humility, crediting the fans, his coaches, and his teammates ahead of his own achievements. He remained positive without being cocky, and he refused to take all the credit for himself.

Ultimately, when I watched Darnold's performance both on the field and off, I saw the power of a positive mindset. Here was someone who figuratively took the weight of the world on his shoulders and carried his underdog team to a surprising and satisfying victory.

WE'RE BRAVE EVEN WHEN WE DON'T KNOW IT

As Darnold's example shows us, the outlook you bring with you can change the course of your life. You're never too young to practice a positive mindset—or to reap the rewards.

Not too long ago, my alma mater, Stony Brook University, asked me to speak with a group of sociology students who would soon graduate. During the discussion, I shared my own experiences as a young sociology major learning how to apply my degree as a professional. While sociology is, without question, a valuable field, its real-world applications aren't always clear.

Ever the optimist, I told them that this ambiguity wasn't a weakness, but rather a strength. As I've discovered, sociologists can apply their degrees in almost any field. I assured them that the door to a fulfilling career, one where they could apply the knowledge they'd built up over the past four years, was wide open for them.

To start the discussion, I asked the thirty-plus students and faculty, "How many people in the room have a 3.0 GPA or higher?" About 90 percent raised their hands. Continuing, I said, "That makes a lot of sense, because that's why you're here. You're overachievers. You want to learn. You want to get more."

Next, I asked how many students would graduate below a 3.0. Only about two or three raised their hands. Not wanting to discourage them, I told them that I too graduated slightly below a 3.0. Driving my point home, I said, "There's no direct correlation between success and grade point average. However, there is a direct correlation between working super hard and success. Sometimes hard work gets you good grades, but good grades on their own do not necessarily guarantee that you'll be successful. I'm proof of that."

I'm sure this message surprised them. After all, from kindergarten through college, maintaining good grades is a student's primary focus. Now, as these undergrads prepared to leave school and set out on their careers, here I was telling them that other things mattered more than their grades.

From there, I described the components of success that I had observed in others and experienced myself. I focused a lot on people, communities, the differences between the haves and the have-nots, and how to give back to the community. Most importantly, I stressed that it was up to them to make opportunities for themselves, and they shouldn't expect anyone to hand them anything because of good grades.

After my talk and the Q&A that followed, the crowd dispersed. A lone student named Christopher timidly walked up to me and introduced himself. "How do you get in front of a room and speak so well?" he asked, adding, "I could never do that."

"How old are you, Christopher?" I said.

"Twenty-four."

"I'm fifty-eight. I've lived life. I've had my ups. I've had my downs. I've had my experiences. I've learned a lot. Because of that, I have a lot to tell you. But here's one thing I could say about you: you're the only one in this room that walked over to me to have this conversation. That tells me a lot about you, Christopher."

He may not have seen himself as a brave go-getter, but I saw a kid who had watched eagerly from the back of the room, who had listened to everything I said over those forty-five minutes, and who was eager to engage me in conversation afterward and learn more.

I told him that, while he didn't have much to share with others yet, I could see he was curious, he would learn from his own experiences in time, and one day he'd share them with others.

Sometimes, we don't see our positive traits or the good we're bringing into the world. Christopher saw himself as shy and incapable of engaging a crowd. I saw a brave, curious person eager to learn and apply those lessons to his career. Everyone else listened to me and left. He saw the opportunity to get more out of the experience, and he took it.

KNOW WHAT MAKES YOU TICK

The way I see it, in both business and life, everybody has to make it in their own way. Whatever you are, whatever you have, use that to your advantage.

If you see yourself as a shy person like Christopher, learn how to use your shyness. Sometimes the brash, outspoken person gets the best results. Sometimes the opposite is true. Whoever you are, learn how your innate traits can help you.

For instance, I know I'm a salesman through and through. By nature, I want to engage people. I think fast and don't do as well in environments where I need to slow down. My strength is my ability to move from one thing to the next, to try and accumulate as many leads and sales as possible.

That's me. I know that not everybody is meant to be a salesman. Fast thinkers aren't smarter than slow thinkers. We just approach ideas and situations differently. Slow thinkers are far better suited to dig deeper. Scientists, for instance, stay on one issue for as much time as it takes to produce an answer. The scientist's mindset is naturally different than mine. After all, scientists don't sell cancer; they cure cancer.

Purely by walking up to me, Christopher showed me that he was different than anyone else in that room. He had a different understanding of himself, and while he may have been a little too self-critical, he clearly wanted to propel himself forward into something greater.

For Christopher, that was a good start. By knowing what makes you tick, you can become more positive, and therefore more proactive. You will learn how to use your skills better, to identify your objectives, and to prepare for the task at hand. There are infinite ways forward in the world, but each of them starts with a firm understanding of who you are and what you're good at.

At one of my companies, Mixology, one of my partners is a creative thinker through and through. In any business conversation having to do with numbers, finances, and the like, you can see him check out. Instead, his mind is on colors, dimensions, and design.

Since we're in the clothing business, we need someone like him, and I've learned to play to his strengths. Jordan gets the columns and the charts, since he's all about budgeting, projections, and discipline. My partner gets the creative prompts, the visionary messages, and the visual stimuli, because that's what he knows, and that's what he's good at. Between the two of them, they make a great team, and they're confident in each other's ability to take care of things on his end.

DREAM THE DREAM—BUT EXECUTE IT

My father is a dreamer. At eighty-nine, he's still shooting off business ideas to my kids. He may have stepped out of the day-to-day of the family business a while ago, but he's still engaged in whatever my kids are up to, especially since he knows they've taken on his legacy.

I like to think that my father would have pursued every one of his business ideas if given the chance. This would have been impractical and pulled him in far too many directions at once, but dreamers don't worry about the logistics. They're too busy coming up with the next big thing.

Fortunately, my mother was his opposite in many ways. Always the practical one, while my father dreamed, my mother did all the little things to make our business stand out. When they called for triage, for instance, she was all over it. You couldn't find a better pair for a developing business.

When I think of my mother's approach, I liken it to a coach drilling down his running back. "Hit the hole between the two and the four," the coach will say, "and keep running that play until they figure out how to stop you." In other words, there's nothing wrong with running the same play over and over again, if it gets you five yards every time.

My mother applied this same mindset in the family laundry business. It all began after World War II, when my father looked at my grandfather's business and saw a new opportunity. At the time, my grandfather owned a laundry service for the wealthy, picking up the dirty laundry from various houses every day, washing it, and then returning it to the housekeepers.

One day, my parents realized that it wasn't just the laundry that needed to get to and from these estates, but the housekeepers as well. Together, my parents set out on their new business venture. They worked out of their apartment, putting flyers on windshields until they got a few customers. Their new business plan was to pick up the housekeepers at their homes in the morning, take them to work, and then bring them back in the evening. No one had ever tried this before. It was such an avant-garde idea that it could be compared to the Amazon of today.

Eventually, they had so many customers that they bought a bus to accommodate all their workers. Through all of it, they kept to the same narrowly defined plan day in and day out. They knew what their clientele wanted, and they executed it well.

Like in the running back analogy, you should only keep doing something until it doesn't work anymore. Then, do something else.

Whenever the time came for their business to evolve, my father, the dreamer, was always ready with an idea for the next step, and then he and my mother would figure out how to execute it. Through the generations, my family's businesses have evolved, but our philosophy has never changed: define what you do, do it consistently, and do it well.

CHRIS BARNARD AND THE POWER OF POSITIVITY

For my business associate Chris Barnard, the power of a positive mindset has roots in the Bible with Proverbs 23:7: "For as a man thinketh in his heart, so *is* he." As Chris put it, "God created man in His image as a 'creator.' If he can see it in his mind, he can do it."

If you approach life with a positive outlook, that doesn't mean your outlook won't be challenged from time to time. Chris recalled one of these moments particularly well:

> *In 2001, I purchased an automotive repair shop from a childhood friend. Going into the business, I saw myself as more righteous than my friend and therefore supposed that the business would grow under my leadership. Within two years, after a poorly executed transition of ownership, I was forced to shut it down and settle to more than $150,000 in debt at a time when that was three-to-five times my annual income. My vision of myself at that moment was one of failure. Rather than settling on that mental image, I looked for lessons I could learn and opportunities I could pursue to maintain my integrity and pay what I owed. I changed my image from failure to a responsible man with integrity. Within two years, an opportunity arose that took me in a new business direction, helped me pay my debts, and has since provided a solid foundation to build on for both me and my son.*

Chris said that if he were to give one piece of advice to an aspiring young leader, it would be that their mindset must be based in truth. In his experience with the auto shop, he saw this play out in a few different ways. "When I saw myself as more righteous than my friend, my arrogance and pride led to a fall, because that was not the truth," Chris said. "I was no more righteous than he. I simply approached things differently."

Chris's inability to see the truth may have led to unforeseen business challenges, but his ultimate embrace of the truth offered him a way out. "If I had stayed in the mindset of failure, I would have never identified or pursued the opportunities that are now the foundation of my prosperity," Chris said, adding, "I was not a failure, I had simply failed at something."

After this realization, Chris said his newfound ability to embrace positivity changed everything for him. "It was only when I saw myself in light of the truth that I could choose to be responsible and walk in integrity. I had the power to overcome my failure and build a foundation for my future. Failure became a stepping-stone to success."

For Chris, his hard-earned success taught him an important business lesson. "A leader must constantly be aware of their mental image on the inside and measure it against the truth," he said. "Truth is not your past experiences. It is not your present circumstances. Truth is your God-ordained potential. Choose to focus on who God created you to become."

ENJOY LIFE'S JOURNEY

In youth sports, every team has a first string and a second string, those who start the game on the field and those who start on the bench. I hated when I didn't get picked for a team or sat on the bench. It pissed me off, in fact.

Even at a young age, however, I realized that I had a choice. I could ride the pines and feel sorry for myself, or I could work harder and get noticed. I chose the latter. Any time I sat out, I made myself a student of the game. I studied every play, I watched how the more successful players carried themselves, and I formulated a plan to get off the bench and back on the field.

There is something about the human spirit that makes some people work harder in the face of adversity. I learned this firsthand on the playing field when I was young, and as I got older, I carried this lesson with me into the professional world.

The truth is, no one gets better overnight. We must plan for the future, setting up as many checkpoints as it takes to turn our goals into reality. Never forget: if life is a long movie, you're the writer, director, and star. To make your movie compelling, you must show the world how you handle yourself in both the good times and the bad.

As you live out the movie of your life, however, remember to enjoy yourself. A positive outlook means taking things as they come and keeping your options open. Sometimes this will mean changing careers, other times it will mean finding a new hobby, and other times still it will mean pulling up stakes and looking for opportunity elsewhere. Commit yourself to whatever it is you're doing in the moment, but embrace opportunity whenever it pops up.

One of my good friends started as an accountant in a big brokerage firm in the 1980s. He worked on the service side of the business, but he longed to get over to the production side as a trader. One day, he got his big opportunity—while taking a leak in the men's room.

As the story goes, he was taking a quick break to relieve himself, when a bigwig from a Wall Street bank came in. My friend may have violated a rule or two of bathroom etiquette in the process, but he managed to strike up a conversation with the guy. Not long after, he was hired on as an entry-level trader for the bank.

I'm sure he would have been an excellent accountant, and he was certainly committed to his work, but it wasn't where his heart was. In the short term, he kept his head down, did his work, and didn't complain. However, the second a better opportunity arose, in the men's room of all places, he took it and never looked back.

Ultimately, his instincts paid off. He rose to head trader at the bank and retired a very wealthy man at thirty-nine.

However, life's journey won't work out quite that way for all of us. I remember talking to another friend of mine, we'll call him Ed, in 2009, when the economy was reeling from the collapse the year before. Before the collapse, he'd been doing unbelievably well in Grand Junction, Colorado. He had everything he wanted: a successful vineyard, a souped-up truck, and a cherry Harley.

Sadly, he bet the ranch on a new housing development right before the real-estate market collapsed, and he lost everything. I remember talking to him in the aftermath. We focused mostly on helping him build a positive mindset, so that he could turn this collapse into a temporary setback and get back on his feet again.

First, I asked him to step outside of his body and his problems. Then, I told him to look himself right in eye and give himself whatever advice he needed to hear.

Finally, I had him identify all the parts of his life that were going well. For a lot of us, when we get down, we tend to focus only on all the things that have gone wrong. The truth is it's rarely ever all bad. In the darker moments of our lives, these bright spots help us carry on, anchoring us, so we can pick ourselves back up and forge ahead.

If you can't do this yourself, meet with someone you trust, and go through your problems with them. It doesn't matter if it's a friend, family member, or mentor. Just talk your problems out with somebody, and see where that takes you. You'll gain a new understanding of both yourself and your problems in the process.

I got to be this guy for Ed. As he likes to say, it was part of my job as a friend. He didn't dig himself out of his hole overnight, but eventually he came back out on top. After cutting his losses with his vineyard in Colorado, he moved to North Dakota and capitalized on the real-estate boom as the oil and gas industries swept in and drilled. Today, he's got a new wife, a new RV, and a renewed appreciation for the twists and turns of life's journey.

EXERCISE: WHAT MAKES YOU TICK?

Just like anything else in life, maintaining a positive attitude takes work and planning. The more resilient you are, and the more willing you are to roll with the surprises and seize opportunity, the stronger your mindset will be. Use the space below to answer the following questions.

1. What makes you tick?

2. Identify things in your life that inspire curiosity, courage, and positivity.

3. List at least three things you can do right now to help you pursue your goals.

MAKE POSITIVITY A CORE VALUE

No two people are going to find success in the same way. In this chapter, I've stressed the importance of identifying and seizing opportunities when they present themselves. How you get there, of course, is up to you.

In the next chapter, we'll talk about the importance of establishing core values in your professional life—things like hard work, ethics, and family. At the center of all this, however, is positivity. If you can consistently embrace an optimistic outlook, all the other core values will fall into place.

As I've always told my kids, if you're not getting up in the morning with a positive attitude, then go back to sleep.

Accomplishing this is a little bit of a balancing act. Here's my suggestion: if you need to be up by seven, wake up at six. That way, if you need the extra hour, you'll feel like you got to sleep in. The best part is that if you do wake up at six, you'll get to see the sun rise, which is the most inspiring part of any day.

To maintain a positive mindset, we all need to adapt in different ways. Further, we must constantly evolve throughout our lives to meet our needs. In my family, we call this process "learning to like fish." I didn't eat fish for the first forty years of my life. I just didn't like it. These days, however, I've come to love fish.

My point is this: you may not like fish now, but you may someday. You may not like waking up early to enjoy the sunrise now, but you may someday. Both in business and in our personal lives, nothing ever stays the same.

I see this all the time. Our real-estate business has seen a remarkable shift in our tenants over the past few years. Where we used to lease larger spaces to established firms, now we're learning to parcel out floor space to accommodate the rise of small, one- or two-person entrepreneurs.

Traditionally, the self-employed have worked from home offices. However, for whatever reason, we've reached a tipping point in recent years. More and more freelancers are leaving the confines of their homes and seeking out public spaces. Luckily for us, we saw where things were headed and adapted our business model accordingly.

Take the rise and fall of the big-box store as another example. Twenty years ago, stores like Macy's, Barnes & Noble, and Home Depot were putting smaller local stores out of business right and left. For a time, they seemed unstoppable, but then ecommerce companies like Amazon showed how vulnerable the big-box stores were.

Today, a funny thing has happened. As Internet shopping takes hold and chain box stores close by the dozen, local vendors are seeing a resurgence. In Greenville, Texas, where we own an office building, I recently read an article about the city's resurgent downtown area. As the city invests in infrastructure, new wine shops, theaters, and clothing stores are popping up to meet new customer demand.

This is happening in cities all over the country where people want to live and work. The Internet may have enabled us to work and shop from home, but as it turns out, we humans are social creatures. More than working and buying stuff, we crave the kinds of tactile, real-world experiences that the Internet can't provide.

As a people, I like to think that we are learning to like fish all over again, reclaiming and revitalizing an older way of doing things to meet our ever-changing needs.

Every time technology and the marketplace conspire to change the way we work, buy, and interact with others, someone is making a fortune on the new opportunity that shift has provided. That someone could be anyone, so why not make it you?

CHAPTER TWO

The Power of Lifelong Values

· · · · ·

In my life, I've always followed the rules. I love rules. Tell me what to do, and I will do it exactly the way you told me. I won't exceed the rules, I won't go into the gray area, and I certainly won't break them. To me, there is no other option; do things the right way, or don't do anything at all.

I wish more business leaders held this belief.

Even in my first job as a newspaper delivery boy when I was six, I was a stickler for doing my job right. My boss would hand me thirty-five to forty papers and tell me to have them all delivered no later than three o'clock.

I didn't just have to do my job quickly, though. I also had to do it well. If any of our subscribers opened a wet newspaper, it meant that I hadn't followed the rules, so I committed myself to keeping the papers dry at all costs.

Flash forward about twenty years. In the late seventies and through the eighties, I worked for my father in the health-care business. For the three-plus decades my father was in business, the industry remained largely unregulated.

By the mid-to-late eighties, that all changed. At the time, the industry was growing rapidly, and reports of fraud, abuse, and declining quality surfaced across the country. Eventually, the Department of Health, the Department of Labor, and Social Services all stepped in, each with their own set of rules for providers like ourselves to follow.

Many of my father's peers in the industry balked at these new regulations. "They can't do that to us!" they'd shout. "They can't just up and change the rules!" Many had been in this business for even longer than my father, some as many as seventy years. They were comfortable with the way things worked and were understandably resistant to change.

However, the writing was on the wall. Watching the sea change at hand, I told my father, "Dad, we have two choices. We either embrace change and follow the rules, or we go out of business. If we fight the system, the system will kill us." Though my father trusted my opinions implicitly, having made me president of the company a few years before, I can't imagine this was easy for him to hear.

Eventually, my prophecy came true. All the players in the industry who decided to dig in their heels and resist either went out of business or became so marginalized that they may as well have. However, because we had embraced change, our business grew faster than it ever had before. Ultimately, as the industry consolidated, we bought out about fourteen of our former competitors who had failed to change with the times.

EMBRACE HARD WORK

Any businessperson will tell you that change is hard work in the short term. It's hard to embrace, especially when you can't see the payoff immediately. The truth is, if you can't see the payoff, and you don't like where your industry is headed, it's okay to say, "I can't do that anymore," and walk away. It doesn't mean you're a failure. It just means that this venture has run its course for you.

If you want to stay in business, however, whatever your industry may be, you've got to embrace the hard work and roll with the changes as they come. Time after time, I've seen it: you either adjust to change and adapt more quickly than your competition, or you resist change and watch someone else grab the glory.

Here's another funny story from my health-care days. Along with the new regulations for our industry, the eighties also brought us radical changes in technology and how we did business. At the time, we were a small company of about twenty employees. We did everything manually, a feat we can marvel at today, but which was commonplace at the time.

As we seized on opportunities for growth, I realized that we would need to update our processes now or endure severe growing pains later. Fortunately for us, my cousin, Steven Kolman, was in the computer-systems business. I told him where we were, what we wanted, and why. However, when he came in to look at our business, he said, "Some companies are meant to use computers, and some companies aren't. You're a small business. You're not meant to be using computers."

From a short-term perspective, all my cousin saw was a big investment with no immediate payoff. He was trying to be helpful, but I knew he was being shortsighted. We needed to do the work now.

With no other choice, I hired someone else to build us an integrated intranet, and soon we became one of the first providers in our industry to embrace digital processes. With other companies lagging, this move helped us grow dramatically.

Doing the hard work is rarely glamorous, but it makes the difference between a successful business and a failed one. More recently, Jordan demonstrated this with our clothing business, Mixology. Initially, my investment in Mixology felt like a sunk cost. I wanted to grow our brand and market share, but we weren't building the kind of momentum we needed to propel ourselves forward.

Our biggest problem in those early years is we weren't running a tight ship. Whether in sales, purchasing, or bookkeeping, we were leaving money on the table and spending more than we needed to.

I brought Jordan in to see if he could help. Right away, he addressed these fundamental problems. He established an efficient, easy-to-track inventory system. He brought in a controller to help with financing. He ordered a thorough review of the books, accounting for every bill, receipt, and payment in the process. He knew that to move Mixology forward, we first had to do the hard work of rebuilding our foundation.

It wasn't easy, and it certainly wasn't glamorous, but it saved the company from near-certain financial ruin. Mirroring our long-held family values, Jordan took Mixology back to the rule book of running a good business, and it worked.

Ultimately, that's what it comes down to. Follow the rules, and your business should prosper. Following the rules can be hard sometimes, but I've never found any downside to doing so.

EMBRACE HONESTY AND INTEGRITY

I also see no downside to being moral, ethical, and good-natured. In fact, I've often found that through honesty, you can disarm people and create opportunities for yourself that you otherwise wouldn't have had.

A lot of people see honesty as a weakness. A lot of salespeople and business owners dwell too often in moral gray areas. They think they must deliberately mislead customers to get their business.

We don't do that at my companies.

As I tell everyone, if someone criticizes you for being ethical, honest, and trustworthy, then let that be your biggest problem. We would rather pass on a business opportunity than mislead our customers.

I've seen plenty of deals fall through because I didn't pay someone off or take a bribe. In those situations, you should ask yourself why you would even want that business in the first place. If you know your business partner isn't trustworthy from the outset, do you think you can count on that person to be so later?

When you meet someone whom you think isn't trustworthy, listen to your instincts. I had an employee, a couple years my senior, who worked for me for more than twenty years, eventually becoming vice president of our company. While many would look at that and say he did well, I saw a person who had flattened out. He had a terrible work ethic, was standoffish to everyone, and repeatedly failed to earn anyone's respect.

This guy would say to me all the time, "Glenn, your greatest fault is that you never fire anybody. You've got to get rid of some of these people." It was an interesting comment coming from a person who rarely met my expectations and generated constant complaints. However, despite what he may have thought, to me, integrity in business means investing in your employees' success, not cutting them loose the moment they let you down.

The truth is that too many business leaders are like this guy, ready to fire everybody every day. I think it's the craziest thing. How can you run a business with nobody working for you? If someone's not meeting your expectations, then lift them up, find out the problem from their perspective, and give them the resources they need to generate a positive impact.

Invest in people, and nine times out of ten, that investment will pay off in spades. Through my ill-tempered former VP, I learned that the person ready to cut everyone else loose is most likely the source of the problem.

I'll never forget the time I heard a person say to me, "I screw people before they screw me." He certainly lived by his motto, screwing over everyone until he'd lost credibility and no one would work with him anymore. The last I heard, he has been out of business for years and unable to land another job.

I've never subscribed to his way of thinking. Every morning, I wake up and promise myself to be positive and honest with everyone I encounter. We pay everyone else before we pay ourselves. We help our employees when they need it, and we give back to our community however we can. We are known for our honesty, and both our employees and customers are incredibly loyal to us as a result.

When I think of how far honesty can get you, I often like to bring up Howard Stern. As anyone who's listened to him knows, Stern has a lot of issues. However, instead of burying them, he's made a whole career out of sharing stories about his shortcomings and his visits to the shrink.

I love the guy, but like a lot of people, I don't always like what he has to say. When this happens, instead of getting indignant or outraged, I turn him off. Stern himself has said he's never compelled anybody to listen.

At any rate, Stern is proof that honesty sells. He's also proof that we don't have to like an honest person or even agree with them. The good thing, however, is that you always know where they stand.

STAND FOR SOMETHING

As a young man, I was very competitive in sports. I was the kind of guy on the basketball team who would scream at everybody else to get into position, and then scream even more when they didn't. The teams I played on weren't bad, but we weren't exactly playoff-caliber either. This didn't matter to me. I just wanted to win.

As my playing days wound down, I took that competitive drive with me into business, where I quickly learned I couldn't simply demand success from my coworkers. It was up to me to lead by example.

Just as my father did before me, I made sure I was the first one in the office and usually the last one to leave. I knew that if I wanted to lead, I had to stand for something. I had to set the standard for everyone around me. I worked to lift my team up by the things I did, not by the things I said.

This experience taught me a lot, but in truth, I never saw any other option. I worked for my father full-time when I was only twenty-two and right out of college. By twenty-eight, I was promoted to president of our family business. Just like Sam Darnold leading USC, I was usually the youngest person in the room. With as many as forty people reporting to me, many easily fifteen years my senior, I could only earn their respect by following the rules, being honest, and modeling the standards for integrity set by my parents.

Because the wheels of business are always in motion, the challenges came quickly. Once, an employee came up to me and said, "I want to write business at Flushing Hospital in Queens, but the head of the social-work department is demanding that we take her to Broadway shows and buy her an expensive television."

"We don't do that," I said. "We'll give them the best service, and we will provide the best home-care workers they can find, but we won't pay off to get the business."

"We're not going to get their business," he said.

"Then we'll be the second, third, or fourth referral source that they use. We won't be the first," I said. "If we win our way back to first, it's going to be based on service and not on kickbacks and payoffs."

At only twenty-eight, I didn't always feel comfortable holding my ground in these situations. However, I knew I had to live up to the example my father set, and I knew that I couldn't just pay lip service to these values and look the other way while my salespeople made shady deals. Whenever I found out an employee was bucking these values, I unfortunately had to show them the door.

Sports fostered both my competitive spirit and my belief in following the rules. Thanks to my father, I dedicated myself to following the rules in business, to doing things the hard way if necessary, and to modeling honesty, ethics, and a sense of fair play in everything I did.

These days, I encourage young professionals to ask themselves what leading with integrity means to them.

Dishonest people like to act as if theirs is the only way, that unethical or illegal dealings are simply part of the status quo.

They're wrong. I've done business with enough honest people to know I'm not the only ethical person out there. If you find yourself in an environment where these kinds of shady dealings are going on, know that you don't have to join in.

In fact, you can help set a new standard for honesty and integrity in your company. Find people whose values align with yours, people you respect and admire. Learn from the finest and the best, not the ones torching their futures for short-term success. Then, when the opportunity arises, embrace a leadership philosophy that would make your mentors proud.

TREAT YOUR EMPLOYEES LIKE FAMILY

To my father, integrity meant treating your employees with the respect they deserved. In so many ways, he showed that he cared about his employees, their families, and their continued success.

One of my favorite examples of this is the handwritten newsletters that he used to photocopy and attach to every paycheck. In each letter, he modeled a way of life for his employees, speaking to the values of saving money, education, and family.

Many of his employees had never received this kind of advice, not even from their own parents. As a result, his role as mentor took on fatherly undertones. These practices ran counter to the predominant thinking during my father's time, especially in the eighties.

Case in point, I remember former Pepsi-Cola CEO John Sculley making headlines for promoting a particularly cutthroat business policy around this time. Every year, he said the company would cut ties with the least productive 10 percent of its employees. The idea wasn't unlike pruning a shrub. To keep your company healthy, you had to cut it back a little every year. Otherwise, if you leave them to grow, everything else underneath dies.

While Sculley earned "CEO of the year" recognition for these practices, I understand that he later realized it was inhumane and felt a tremendous sense of guilt for what he did.

Through my father's handwritten newsletters, company picnics, and holiday parties, my father taught me to take a radically different approach: to lift each of your employees up and support them when they struggle, not fire them. As I often say, treat your employees like customers, and you'll have great employees.

When you invest in your employees, you win. I've seen firsthand the kinds of bonds my parents forged—and today, I proudly watch my children do the same. I know people who haven't seen my parents in twenty-five years but still sing their praises. When my mother passed, people we hadn't seen in a decade or more showed up to pay their respects. The experience warmed my heart, and I was grateful that my own children could witness the tremendous results of a lifetime spent trying to do the right thing.

ADHERE TO YOUR VALUES AND BE CONSISTENT

In business and life, we must adhere to our values. After all, they make us who we are and impact all our relationships with others. My dear friend, Rabbi New, knows firsthand the importance of values in leadership. In fact, he always says, "Leadership is essentially about values, deeply rooted convictions, and the moral courage to both defend them and promulgate them."

Rabbi New noted that we all work to follow certain deeply held beliefs, whether those beliefs are intuitive, religious, or otherwise. Each day, as we're challenged to follow and uphold those beliefs, the best leaders help us stay on the path. "The leader is both an anchor who keeps us from drifting away from our values and a captain who has the vision to keep us moving forward, growing, and progressing," Rabbi New said. "The ultimate testament of leadership is not in having many followers, but in empowering others to become leaders in their own right."

Naturally, a rabbi's work involves constant leadership, which often includes settling grievances. In our discussion, Rabbi New recounted a recent dispute between two people with whom he had close personal ties. He was unsure of whether to get involved and risk compromising his relationships or to play it safe and stay out of the fray. Realizing he needed guidance on how to approach the matter, he turned to his wife, who convinced him to do the right thing. "Seeking advice from your spouse," he added, "is always the right thing."

To young professionals interested in growing their own leadership, Rabbi New gave this advice: "Context and proper perspective as to the space business belongs in our lives is paramount. Namely, it is a means and not an end." Even when you're focused on your professional life, Rabbi New stressed that your highest core values should be faith, family, and community. Business, he said, simply helps to support and strengthen those values.

According to the Talmud, the first question we are asked in Heaven is whether we dealt honestly in business. "If that's the first question you're asked," he said, "it is probably because it is the greatest challenge." To meet this challenge and create a business culture where everyone thrives, infuse honesty, integrity, reliability, and respect into all your interactions, from big clients to janitors tasked with keeping your office clean.

At the end of the day, Rabbi New said good leadership comes down to belief in yourself and your abilities. After all, "If what you believe is true, it will resonate with others." However, New stressed that good leaders do more than believe. They are proactive, not reactive. "You've gotta hustle to the best of your G-d-given ability," Rabbi New said, "and leave the rest to G-d."

To Rabbi New's advice, I would add one other component into your values tool kit: be consistent. Think how you can achieve consistently high performance both in your job and at school. What leaders do you admire who have proven that they aren't one-hit wonders, that they have what it takes to succeed time after time?

When you're consistent, you're far better prepared to raise the bar, to take your goals to the next level. In school, doing well means getting a better job or having your pick of graduate schools. As a young professional, it means something else entirely. Perhaps it's money, or perhaps it's the freedom to travel the world.

Throughout my life, I've heard that certain people are born to lead. I've never seen it that way. Leaders are born out of hard work, consistency, and the drive to never rest on their laurels. Wherever you are in your life, make it your goal to accumulate as many victories as you can this year, and then determine how you can build on them for next year.

EXERCISE: WHAT ARE YOUR VALUES?

Now that you've seen some of my values, how I learned them, and what they mean to me, it's your turn. Use the space below to answer the following questions.

1. What's important to you?

2. Who do you know who has strong values? What are their values, and how do they model those values to others?

3. How will your values flow between your personal
    and your professional lives? What challenges can you
    foresee, and what can you do now to address them?

YOUR VALUES FORM THE FOUNDATION
OF YOUR STRATEGY

As we forge ahead to the next chapter, remember that the
values you identify aren't just something you recite, but
something you live by. If fact, good businesses embed
their values directly into their identity. Take the following
mission statement, courtesy of Jordan at Mixology:

Be trustworthy and live in the present.

Create!

*Create happiness, health, and prosperity for all
living things.*

Teach and give.

*Teach and mentor the able, and give to those who cannot
help themselves.*

Keep balance in all things.

Pay attention to the details, but never lose sight of the big picture.

If you don't take risk, you cannot win.

Be prepared to be unprepared.

Now, take a look at Mixology's core values:

We treat our people like customers.

We do not cut corners.

We pay our vendors, landlords, and service providers first.

We get better and better every day.

People do business with people. Treat them well.

Radiate positivity.

What's wrong is always available, and so is what's right.

Take extreme ownership.

Invest in loss.

Throughout the next chapter, ask yourself: why shouldn't my core values be incorporated into my business strategy? Why are business students taught to keep these things separate when they don't need to be?

Most professionals are incapable of marrying their values with their business strategy. Not coincidentally, most businesses fail in the first five years. Naturally, economic and financial factors are always at play, but so much of it comes down to a lack of ethics and integrity.

Once you taste success, don't get complacent. Work harder. Keep being the first person to show up and the last person to leave. Stay involved. Know what your employees are doing, and ask how you can help them. Treat your employees like customers—and always treat your customers right.

Believe in the power of lifelong values. It may not feel like it, but they do work. Look at all the major religions. They haven't changed their playbooks in thousands of years. Instead, they keep reinforcing their core values year after year, because the more we hear them, the more we learn how to apply them to our own lives.

CHAPTER THREE

The Power of a Keen Strategy

· · · · ·

You have to know what you stand for before you lay out your game plan. Otherwise, you have nothing to build your strategy around. Successful business leaders first go into business with products and teams they believe in. Then, they set up a series of short-term and long-term goals to get there.

Setting all this up is the easy part. The real key to a successful game plan is preparation. This is especially apparent in sports. If you don't put in the work ahead of time, if you don't do all that you need to before you hit the field, you lose your shot. At best, you might be able to make a short-term stab at victory, but the second your competition catches you faking it, they will pull ahead.

I see businesses make this mistake all the time in social-media marketing. Too often, they'll set superficial goals—such as getting a million likes—rather than actually generating engagement.

However, if these likes aren't leading to sales, then what's the point? One of the biggest social-media stars out there, Kim Kardashian, generates tons of likes. The difference is that she doesn't fake it; she and her team have a proven engagement strategy. That's how she sells hundreds of millions of dollars' worth of goods. I may not be able to relate to her, but I certainly admire the business she's built.

At Mixology, we've come a long way in this regard. After making major investments in our website, trying to create a buzz, the sales weren't coming fast enough to justify the effort. We knew that social media could be good for a clothing brand, but as Jordan says, our business should be judged by sales and customer satisfaction. Buying artificial likes will not build our business, so we invest our resources elsewhere.

Ultimately, your goals and your strategy must align. Generating authentic likes might be a decent enough short-term goal, but you can't ignore the endgame. Even more, you can't sit back for even one day. Once you've seen some success, how will you adjust your strategy to create even more?

TWO STEPS BACK, ONE LEAP FORWARD

My parents had trouble finding quality workers in the early days of their housekeeping business. In the 1950s, no other businesses like theirs existed. The idea of recruiting and transporting housekeepers as a standard delivery service was brand new—and all their own. This gave them a great competitive advantage, but it also meant they had to create the template as they went along.

Further, because they were an unknown quantity, they didn't attract a big talent pool at first. This unfortunately saddled them with a subpar group of workers and hurt their ability to build a strong customer base. You can make all the excuses in the world, you can even give away free service, but if that service isn't very good, then even free isn't cheap enough.

Struggling to move forward, my parents first took two gigantic steps backward. It may not sound like it, but this was a sound strategic move. They realized that if they wanted to grow their business properly, they first had to scale down their client load and focus on delivering quality service.

For a while, they only sent out a handful of workers they could trust. With each new hire, they focused on building quality employees and scaling their business up from there.

The strategy paid off. Many members of this core group stayed on to work for my parents for thirty or forty years.

To capture the wisdom of this approach, my parents adapted a motto: "Only deliver the cream of the crop." By insisting on quality employees, their business took off as a result of the phenomenal word of mouth they received.

Here's one good thing about word of mouth that a lot of businesses don't talk about: a good reputation doesn't just get you good customers, but also good employees. This, combined with the care my parents put into making every employee feel valued—serving them coffee in the office, hosting company barbecues, and sharing unexpected gifts with workers—built a culture of employees who cared about what they were doing, because they knew they were cared for.

This strategy is fairly common today, but in the fifties, sixties, and seventies, especially in the housekeeping industry, my parents' approach was the exception, not the rule. In any era, doing a great job and treating everybody with dignity may not sound like much, but it sure gets you a long way.

Everyone loved my parents and reflected that love in their work. I consider that one of the most important lessons I've ever learned from them.

Ultimately, two steps back became an endless march forward, and their business eventually became the largest provider of housekeepers in New York. They were trailblazers at the time, but today there are plenty of maid services built off my parents' model.

STICKING TO THE GAME PLAN

Especially in family business, another great benefit of the people-first approach is the generational impact it creates.

I worked in my parents' office when I was twelve or thirteen. Not too long after, when I was no older than fifteen, I was already honing my salesmanship skills with customers. A little after that, I helped run the office on occasion.

I watched my parents focus on a specific strategy and stick to it. I like to say that I was taught by osmosis. It's not an unusual story; a lot of kids learn the ropes of business from their parents, just as a lot of kids grow up to take over the family business, which I eventually did.

By modeling these skills for me so relentlessly, my parents didn't only teach me responsibility. They also ensured that their legacy was in good hands when it came time to pass the business on to me.

Through my parents' mentorship, I learned that there's only one option: integrity. All strategy builds out from that, impacting the workplace at a fundamental level. Every office I've ever run has been honest, open, and committed to delivering great service. I know it sounds basic, but the people I mentor are surprised at how many applications this simple strategy has.

BEGIN WITH THE END IN MIND

I was taught to know what I wanted in business. Even today, when I go to the office, I have a plan. I don't show up and say, "Let's see what happens today." If you're on my team, you already know the plan—find new clients— and you're already making it happen.

In May 1980, I went to work for my father the day after finishing college, a day that will be engrained in my mind for the rest of my career. At the time, we worked out of a 450-square-foot office staffed with four employees, two of which were part-timers. Countless housekeepers and nurse's aides filed in throughout the day as well, leaving us packed tighter than a clown car.

By the time I sold the business in 2005, we had twenty-five offices and more than six thousand field service workers. We enjoyed fifty years of continuous growth, weathering every recession like it was the coming and going of the tide. My parents started with one customer, and we finished with about twenty thousand.

Sometimes I feel like Ricky Bobby from *Talladega Nights*. In that movie, Will Farrell's character learned an important lesson from his father: "If you ain't first, you're last."

My father had a similar saying: "You're either growing or you're shrinking." Maintaining the status quo is never good enough. Even today, we take this approach both at Mixology and in our real-estate business.

To push this growth forward, you need a certain kind of leader. I like to say that companies usually go with one of two kinds of CEOs: the process-oriented financial expert interested in expanding margins, or the sales-oriented marketer interested in top-line growth. Like my father before me, I come from the latter camp. Not only do I want new customers coming into new locations, but I also want to maximize the selling potential of the locations I already have.

However, while I may constantly work toward this end, I understand that a CEO can't drive this growth alone. Good leaders know that the path to consistent, recession-proof growth starts with finding qualified people—whether their focus is sales or operations. Every business needs both of these core competencies to succeed, but I always joke that without sales, there's no business to operate.

At Mixology, Jordan certainly takes a more operations-based approach than I've tended to, though he still shares my love of driving sales. In many ways, his approach embodies my philosophy that operations support sales.

Before Jordan came in, Mixology experienced considerable growing pains because, although things were improving on the sales side, we didn't have the right people in place to support the increased demand.

Jordan made it his first order of business to fill those spots. First, he hired an inventory manager. Second, he hired a professional buyer for our merchandise. Third, he hired a bookkeeper to make sure our finances were in order across our locations. Finally, he hired a regional manager to ensure operations were consistent across stores. With the right people in place, Jordan has demonstrated that good leaders don't pray for growth; they create the conditions for it.

VISUALIZE THE GOAL, AND LOSE ALL DISTRACTIONS

As a person with ADD, I am living proof that anyone can rise above distractions, learn how to focus, and get the job done. No matter how your brain processes things, you just have to make it work for you.

In sales, I find that my jumping from lead to lead or idea to idea helps as long as I remember to keep my end goal in mind. I often find myself multitasking, working a variety of leads simultaneously.

To the outside observer, it may look chaotic. For me, however, it keeps me focused. I don't let things lapse. I make sure that everything I'm doing keeps me working toward a singular goal. If that goal is to open more clothing stores in New Jersey over the next few years, then all the leads I cultivate will be in service of that goal.

Good leaders know how to hold both themselves and their teams accountable to the company goals. To keep that focus, you must constantly repeat your message, so it becomes part of the ongoing conversation surrounding your business operations.

Business meetings sometimes get a bad rap as time-wasters, but I've found them to be excellent forums for setting goals and renewing focus. At Mixology, senior leadership meets every week to check in with each other, and then they immediately meet with their own management teams afterward to disseminate the message.

We also couple this with constant formal and informal training. I've been a hands-on leader in all of my companies, because I enjoy the communication with my employees. The benefits go both ways. I get to listen and learn from the employees who are actually carrying out our goals, and in turn those employees get to see that, as leaders, we're focused on the prize and looking to improve our execution.

There's a certain repetition to all of this, but the beauty of repetition is that it reaffirms the idea that everybody from the top down is working toward the same goal.

Though I'm a big believer in meetings, visualization, and goal-setting, here's a warning: never schedule your meetings during peak business hours.

After all, why would you take people out of their day-to-day routines during peak hours if you're trying to build a successful business?

Goals are great, but they should never distract from your ability to execute. If your peak hours fall between 11:00 and 3:30, you should be working during that time and supporting your team in whatever capacity you can.

How you approach this will depend on your industry and routine. At one of my former companies, I made sure all vendors visited me either before or after the normal workday. I told them that if they wanted to sell their service to me, it couldn't take me away from running my business.

This didn't always go over well. Often, the conversation would go something like this: "Come by at 7:30," I'd say.

"Really?" They'd often reply. "How about I show up at 6:30?"

I remained steadfast. "Come in at 7:30, and I'll meet with you. If you try to come during the day, I can't see you."

Today, my business and scheduling needs are different. I needed to focus on running my business during operating hours back then. Today, I often meet with vendors over lunch.

HAVE A PLAN FOR MAKING MONEY

I consider Terry Lundgren, the outgoing CEO of Macy's, one of the greatest retail businessmen of our era—despite a falling stock price and recent store closures. Recently, I listened to him speak about the impact of ecommerce and changing consumer habits on his department stores and found his comments insightful.

First, he pointed out that, while Macy's may be closing some stores, their Internet business is growing rapidly. However, as he pointed out, 90 percent of people still shop in stores and malls. Contraction is one thing, but in both his experience and my own with Mixology, it's hard to imagine a future where the physical clothing store completely disappears. Ecommerce may grow its 10-percent slice of the customer pie, but it will never be the whole pie.

As leaders, it's important that we anticipate and understand these kinds of changes. Even more importantly, we also need to understand how our competition is responding. As an example, Lundgren pointed to the amount of web-based companies running their businesses at a loss by essentially giving things away for free.

Short-term, there could be some sense to this, but this is no way to run a business long-term. If you don't have a plan for making money, how can you ever have an endgame?

A few years ago, Gilt was one of the fastest-growing Internet companies in the country, raising about a half-billion dollars in start-up money and generating somewhere between $200 and $300 million in sales.

Not surprisingly, the company was valued at over a billion dollars at the time. In so many ways, they were poised to make a big splash in Internet-based retail. After a couple of years, they weren't making any money. Despite raising all the capital and generating a big buzz, they couldn't convert that goodwill into profit, and things went south.

Soon, the Hudson Bay Company, which owns Saks Fifth Avenue, bought Gilt for about $200 million, well below the equity that went into it. I'm sure the equity players were happy to get their thirty-, forty-, or fifty-cent return on the dollar once it was clear Gilt wasn't going to survive as a standalone entity, but it probably goes without saying that everyone was expecting a lot more from the company.

Ultimately, Gilt fell victim to the bottom line: you have to make money to stay in business.

This all goes back to having a solid, workable game plan. I've seen too many venture capitalists dump money into companies that have good ideas but no plan for turning them into revenue or profit. Investing in such a company goes against everything I believe in business.

It's too bad that so many companies make this mistake. The great thing about the Internet is that it has no barriers to entry. Young people could start a business from their dorm if they wanted, and many do.

To get their name out there, they could incentivize customers with some free stuff. However, if they don't plan ahead, if they don't take a look at their margins and determine when they have to charge and how much, they're not going to be in it for the long haul. As I learned from my parents, if building a profitable organization means pulling back and selling less, then so be it.

A couple of years ago, Mixology had to do precisely this. Our Internet division was growing like a weed. Unfortunately, the orders were coming in so fast that we didn't have enough inventory. We ended up fulfilling only about 65 to 70 percent of our orders, which is no way to run a successful business if you want to maintain a good reputation.

Things couldn't keep going in that direction, and after some soul-searching, we decided to take a big step back so that we could make sure we did things the right way.

Today, we fulfill 99.9 percent of every online order we get. Not only is the inventory always there, but so is the customer service and the packaging. By pulling back, we've built a system that can last and that can grow to meet increasing demand.

At this point, you might be wondering about Amazon, the two-thousand-pound gorilla in the retail room. After all, Amazon is famous for selling products below cost simply to undercut their competition and gain business. However, Amazon has learned how to do this sustainably. They have a plan for making money. Recently, that plan has been to open a couple hundred physical stores because they see where the market is headed.

Malcolm Gladwell talks about this kind of phenomenon in his book *The Tipping Point*. Things can only head in one direction for so long before something happens to change it. Amazon may have driven the ecommerce revolution, but they see the tipping point coming; they know that people miss the experience of brick-and-mortar shopping, and Amazon wants in on the action.

No matter how the revenue works out for them exactly, Amazon knows, just as we do at Mixology, that the future holds great opportunity for boutique shopping experiences. Your web business can be both a great moneymaker and a great place to offer deals, but long-term you may need to be thinking about more.

For us, we see our physical stores as a way to build stronger relationships so our customers think of us whether they're shopping online or in person. We want them to know who we are, what we stand for, and that we are honorable and loyal to our customers.

WRITE EVERYTHING DOWN

When I was younger, I used to carry around one of those Filofax folders everywhere I went. It was as thick as a paperback book, and it still didn't hold everything I wanted it to, but it was my life. Eventually I upgraded to a loose-leaf binder, and then to a smartphone.

Whatever I'm using at the time, I write everything down. I do mean everything—from the kinds of inspirational thoughts that have made it into this book to reminders to listen to my favorite music at night. When you're busy, you have a lot of ideas you can't explore in the moment. If you don't have a way of keeping track of them, eventually you'll forget them.

Everyone has their own way of keeping their thoughts organized, some better than others. To this day, my father is an idea man. He's always coming up with a million new schemes, many of which are quite difficult to launch. In the early days, it was my job to try and record all *his* thoughts and try to wrangle them into something that would work.

These days, I only have to keep track of my own thoughts, a process that has certainly evolved over time.

I've often said over my career that you become a lot smarter when you're successful. In reality, you're no smarter. You just feel more confident. You've had your successes and know you can accomplish more. In this regard, while I used to write down whatever came to mind, these days I focus on the thing I think I could actually do. I'm better at weeding out wasteful ideas.

This weeding out skill will develop over time. For now, I encourage aspiring leaders to dream as big as they can and try anything out they think might work. After all, there's no sense limiting yourself before you've tasted success. Over time, you'll get a sense of which ideas are valuable and which ones will lead you down a road with no reward.

Admittedly, it's a balancing act. Dreamers love to dream, and I love them for it. However, at some point we all come to realize that we have limited time for the things we love, and we should focus our energies on the ideas most likely to pay off.

My mother used to say, "Don't look at things you can't afford." My approach to pursuing ideas is the same. Write it all down and think big, but only pursue the things you know you can get done. Further, take heart that all those small things you accomplish over time will eventually grow into something much larger.

As a fundamental strategy, writing things down has great payoffs. It gives you a sense of accomplishment as you work to grind out daily goals, just as it helps you keep an eye on your long-term goals and know that you're making progress.

Whether in business or in sports, it's the same. In business, you don't have just one order to fulfill. In sports, you don't play just one game. If you're the Patriots in the 2017 Super Bowl, you can't come back from one of the largest deficits in Super Bowl history in one scoring drive. You have to set incremental goals that add up to a larger goal.

You can find this story in many of sports' greatest come-backs. Facing seemingly overwhelming odds, the coaches will say, "Just get me one goal back. We're down by thirty; get me ten." It may not always work, but however you look at it, it's the only way forward.

Even if you don't make it all the way back, something can be said for losing by ten rather than by thirty. It's still a loss, but the lessons learned in how you fought back will give you new ideas to try out next time.

Business is a little more forgiving in this way, as we rarely encounter win-or-lose stakes. It's okay to try and convert thirty customers in a day and fall short of that goal. So what if you've only gotten ten or twenty? You made forward progress, and you didn't quit before you started.

In some ways, this comes back to that idea of taking two steps back to take big leaps forward. Write down your ideas and pursue as many as you can, but know sometimes you have to throw up the white flag.

When that day comes, know it's no great shame. Just as I've had my successes, I've had my failures. I've pursued plenty of ideas I thought were going to pan out that didn't.

A lot of times, the warning signs will pop up early. Maybe your employees don't see value in what they're doing, your customers aren't satisfied with the product, or you're simply not turning a profit. If you believe in what you're doing, then you may want to fight through it, but remember sometimes it's okay to pull the plug.

By that same token, know that even the good ideas take time. That's why writing down your next steps, or your next bits of inspiration, are so important. Many businesses don't become profitable for three or four years—sometimes longer. In the meantime, if you're not pushing yourself forward with new ideas to innovate, then those first few years are going to feel like an eternity.

THE STORY OF MIXOLOGY

To see how these little ideas accumulate into something bigger over time, let's take a look at how Mixology grew into what it is today.

When my daughter, Gabrielle, was thirteen, she decided she was no longer interested in organized sports. After announcing her decision to us, I said, "If you're not going to play soccer, you've got to go get a job."

"Who's going to hire me?" she said.

"Don't worry about getting hired," I replied. "Work for free if you have to. Do anything, but you're not sitting at home every day. You've got to be productive."

We weren't trying to be hard on her, but we were committed to raising responsible, disciplined children.

Soon, Gabby worked for free at one of my wife's friend's shoe stores, which in turn was housed within a larger clothing store about a half-mile from our home. Every day, my daughter would head down there after school, and we quickly discovered she was every bit the natural salesperson that I was.

The shoe concession went away after about a year, but the couple that ran it, the Shapiros, were so impressed with Gabby that they asked her to come over to their clothing store, a high-end shop with about a thousand square feet of retail space.

So began Gabby's first real job, and by fifteen or sixteen, the Shapiro family entrusted her with running their stores on the weekends when they weren't around. She stayed on with them all through high school, and they treated her like family.

The economic collapse of 2008 hit the Shapiro family and their two stores hard. With consumer confidence barely registering a heartbeat, sales vanished, and the couple decided to close down one of their stores.

Since they had a lot of inventory to liquidate, they held a big blowout sale. To their surprise, lines were out the door. That's when inspiration hit. The Shapiros realized people still wanted to shop, and they still wanted the boutique store experience, but they wanted to do so on a budget.

While the Shapiros saw incredible opportunity in this emerging fast-fashion industry, they didn't have the money to replace their inventory or remake the store.

This is how I came into the picture. Through my daughter, the Shapiros knew I enjoyed investing in promising businesses, so they came to me with their vision for rebranding as Mixology and asked if I could help.

I was hesitant. Despite my daughter's relationship with them, I hardly knew the Shapiros, and I had very little confidence that a relaunched retailer could succeed in the middle of a recession.

Thankfully, Lisa wouldn't tolerate turning them down after all they'd done for our daughter, so she took it upon herself to invest in the business and get them back on their feet.

With a new model, new merchandise, and significantly lower price points, the store was a tremendous hit.

The timing and concept of Mixology was perfect: take a nice item, such as a pocketbook or a nice pair of shoes, and pair it with fashionable, less-expensive items.

Despite my initial hesitation, I couldn't help but get involved once I understood what they were all about. Further, I knew that while they had hit upon a tremendous business model, they needed help on the implementation side of things.

At this point, the core Edwards family strategy kicked in. I looked at Mixology, I looked at the Shapiro family, and I said, "Well, if you're not growing, you're shrinking."

Not long after, we opened a second store, and then a third. By the time Hurricane Sandy touched down in the Northeast in 2012, we were up to six stores.

The hurricane turned out to be a disaster for our business, but it was a much-needed wakeup call. Before the hurricane, we had stocked up on our fall inventory. After the hurricane, no one wanted to shop. On top of that, two of our stores flooded and didn't get power back for two months.

At this point, I realized we needed help. I was heavily invested in Mixology, but my primary business was, and remains, real estate. Further, while John Shapiro, who ran the day-to-day of the business, was phenomenally creative and a gifted salesman, he did not have the background or experience to manage an operation of this size in the face of crisis.

We both believed in Mixology, however, and we wanted to keep the company running. Since I was unable to give it the attention it deserved myself, I asked Jordan to come in and help right the ship.

Here again, another core Edwards family strategy came into play: sometimes you need to take two steps back in order to take a leap forward.

Jordan looked at the finances in the wake of Hurricane Sandy and decided we needed to shut down three of our six stores if we wanted to stay afloat. Then, he set about rebuilding the company's infrastructure to ensure that when the next storm hit—whether literal or figurative—it wouldn't be our death knell.

Part of that process meant building and expanding our web business. At this point, an abandoned business project from the past ended up being the best path forward for our future.

Some years before, Jordan and Tyler started a web-based business selling remanufactured toner cartridges. I backed them on the effort and helped them build out the site and advertise his services. Unfortunately, despite looking promising, the venture never took off. For every ten dollars they spent in ads, they only brought in about nine dollars in new revenue.

Once again, I looked to the Edwards family playbook and realized since they didn't have a good plan for making money, they were better off putting up the white flag and moving on to something else.

The toner cartridge business didn't work, but nevertheless, it created new opportunity. A year later, Jordan and Tyler had the know-how and established infrastructure to jump-start Mixology's web business.

Throwing my two sons into the pool once again, I told Jordan and Tyler that they had until the end of the summer to convert their old toner site into Mixology's new web business. Sure enough, from the lessons learned at Toner Central, they got it done before Tyler left for his first year of college in September.

Today, the Mixology website is as professional as any other in the clothing business, and Mixology continues to open new stores. It wasn't always a perfect march forward, but by following the Edwards family playbook, we built a company that could last and continue to grow.

EVERY DAY IS A NEW BEGINNING

These days, Jordan Edwards throws himself into the pool without any prompting. A passionate leader is always adding new tools to build Mixology, Jordan will be the first to tell you he's learned how to swim as president on the job.

His biggest lesson? When it comes to strategy, an open mindset and a deep commitment to your team is key.

To accomplish these goals, Jordan applies two Japanese approaches called *shoshin* and *kaizen* to everything he does. "These two concepts help keep me focused and humble," Jordan says.

Shoshin roughly translates to "beginner's mind." As Jordan says, "The older we get, the harder it becomes to keep learning. The glass becomes full, and our life and emotional baggage dulls our youthful ambitions. Shoshin reminds me to approach each day and each task as a beginner would, with no mind and no ego."

While my father has always stressed growth in business, Jordan uses the concept of shoshin to apply that same growth mentality first to his mind before he applies himself to whatever business task is at hand.

At Mixology, this philosophy turns up in interesting ways. "Success leaves clues," Jordan often tells his teams, encouraging them to keep learning and asking questions to figure out how they can do a better job. He also uses shoshin to help keep his employees calm and centered. "Do not get frustrated when things happen, whether floods, rodents, or power outages," Jordan says. "These things happen everywhere and to everyone."

The other concept, kaizen, means "daily change for the better." Jordan says, "I wake up every day and try to do just a little bit better than the day before. There are ups and downs, but each mistake is a lesson to help me grow."

Elaborating on this concept, Jordan uses the analogy of the snowman who started as a snowflake. "You must roll and roll, and keep rolling. Sooner or later, that snowflake will turn into a snowman," Jordan says. "Just like life, we keep rolling, getting better, and learning along the way."

Jordan says, when used in concert, shoshin and kaizen are powerful tools in anyone's personal and professional arsenal. Ultimately, they help promote an ownership mentality, a sense that we are in charge of what happens in our lives and our jobs.

At Mixology, Jordan constantly sees his commitment to these concepts pay off. "I am so proud of everyone's passion and love for their company and stores," he says. As you will see in our discussion of discipline in the next chapter, this mindset of constant ownership and renewal is essential for realizing your goals.

EXERCISE: WHAT ARE YOUR CORE STRATEGIES?

Just like anything else worth doing, creating a strong, foundational strategy takes hard work and planning. But the more work you put in up front, the more those efforts will pay off down the road. Use the space below to answer the following questions.

1. How do you generate ideas?

2. What do you do with them?

3. How can you move from idea to action?

4. What does beginning with the end in mind mean to you, and how can you apply this principle to your business?

FINAL TIP: BACK GOOD PEOPLE

As we wrap up this chapter, I'll leave you with one last strategy. It's important to begin with the end in mind and to have a plan for making money. However, it all begins with backing good people.

Mikky Lessard helps run the MarketPlace for me at my properties in Springfield, Massachusetts. Her new business is just getting started, and I've helped subsidize her efforts with rent relief, some Mixology inventory on consignment, and my own mentorship.

At her company, Simply Grace, their reason for being extends well beyond making money. She and her partner, Nancy Feth, use Simply Grace to give back to the community by revitalizing the business district in Springfield. Along with Simply Grace, the ladies also run a yoga studio and a gift shop, and they also collaborate with other small businesses in order to create a new community in an underserved part of town.

I believe in her business model, but more importantly, I believe when downtown Springfield blossoms into a new renaissance, she and her efforts will be identified as one of the turning points that made it happen.

MGM may be investing hundreds of millions of dollars in a casino across the street from my properties, but these women are doing things the Paul Revere way—person to person, block by block, and always from the heart.

Marcus Lemonis on MSNBC likes to say, "It's people, process, product." Truly, that's the essence of strategy.

At the end of the day, however, it comes down to people. It doesn't matter what your plans are or what you're selling if you don't take responsibility for what you do and put in the energy, commitment, and tenacity to get things done.

We'll talk about the importance of discipline in the next chapter. As you learn these concepts, remember that being disciplined is not the same as being rigid in strategy.

The most successful leaders know how to adjust along the way. When the wind is at their back, they do one thing. When it's in their face, they do another. This doesn't mean the people, product, or process have to change dramatically—it doesn't even mean your goals have to change—but it does mean that you might need to revisit *how* you're approaching those other elements.

That's where the discipline comes in. I'm an old-fashioned guy who believes nothing has fundamentally changed in regard to creating success. You have to commit to what you're doing, and you have to show up ready to act on that commitment every day.

The paths we take to building success can change. The technology can change. The ways we interact with customers, vendors, and employees can change. Our discipline, however, can't.

Technology has allowed modern professionals to accomplish things in a day that used to take six months. Despite this, the percentage of highly successful people relative to population hasn't changed. We still have to commit to getting the job done.

At the end of the day, only a select few have the drive, motivation, discipline, and core values to persevere and succeed. Those are the kinds of people I want to work with and invest in.

CHAPTER FOUR

The Power of Relentless Discipline

· · · · ·

In ninth grade, I stood nearly six feet, four inches tall; weighed about 165 pounds; and wanted to run the quarter mile in track and field. Up to that point, in my junior-high career, I was consistently winning races. After my rapid growth, however, I was no longer ideally suited for this kind of competition, and I found myself losing race after race.

The experience was disheartening, as I'd grown quite used to success as a young athlete. Seeing I was struggling, my coaches suggested I try the high hurdles, a competition better suited to my tall and lanky frame.

I wasn't used to the hurdles, but I trained endlessly, working with my coach to rein my body in and become the star hurdler I knew I could be. By my senior year, I became the third-best high hurdler in Nassau County, setting numerous records at my school—some of which I'm told still stand today.

In those four years running the high hurdles, I learned a lot about discipline, and I've carried those lessons with me throughout my career.

One thing I've learned is that discipline cannot be relegated to one aspect of your life. Good leaders are disciplined in all aspects of their lives, whether it's exercising, spending time with family, or your job.

I tell everyone who will listen that if you plan to do something, plan to do it well. By far, the best way to do this is by establishing a routine and sticking to it.

This doesn't mean you have to be perfect. For instance, exercise and diet mean a lot to me. I don't always meet my goals in this regard, but I keep trying.

In this way, real discipline is often a work in progress. I've worked hard at physical fitness for thirty or forty years and have remained committed to the effort regardless of the results. I see everything in life as a work in progress. Don't quit if you disappoint. Start over the next day, and see what happens.

A rabbi friend of mine once said, "Even though you only come on the high holidays, I'm not chasing you out of this temple, because I'd rather see you occasionally than not see you at all." This philosophy has stuck with me ever since. Instead of quitting because you faltered in your efforts, remind yourself that you have a chance to try again the next day.

Of course, this is different than giving yourself permission to be horrible one day and then trying to make up for it the next. A lapse in discipline doesn't relieve you of your core values, morals, and ethics. It means you're human and you're trying.

RACING AGAINST FAILURE

In chapter 3, I shared my father's saying for business: if you're not growing, you're shrinking. Just as it takes discipline to run the hurdles, it takes discipline to wake up every day and expect more out of yourself.

Since I'm naturally competitive, I like to think of this as my race against failure. I'm not afraid of failure, and I don't see failure as some scary creature chasing after me. Rather, we're both running toward success, and every day I dedicate myself to not letting failure win out.

Here's why this mindset matters. When you're afraid of failure chasing you, you're likely to panic and run yourself off a cliff. That isn't going to help anyone.

Instead, if you see failure as competition, you realize it's something you can beat. This mindset keeps you optimistic. You're no longer trying to escape something; you're trying to reach something instead.

FIND SOMEONE YOU RESPECT

I admit I've had to reign in my competitive nature over the years. I'm a better team player than I was in my sporting days. I don't yell at my team when I think failure is gaining on us. Instead, I remind myself we have more games to play, more chances to press our advantage.

Part of the reason for this mindset is that I learned the value of good coaches and mentors from a young age. Even today as I'm running my race against failure, I try to follow the examples of the people I admire and replicate their most positive attributes.

To find good mentors, look for people who aren't merely successful, but also respected. Whatever one may think of her politics, Meryl Streep tends to fit that mold. She has found incredible success throughout her career, but also the respect and admiration of her entire industry. No one says a bad word about how she conducts herself as a person.

Contrast that with another Hollywood icon, Mel Gibson, who is also phenomenally successful, but disliked by many. Gibson's past remarks and behavior are well documented, so I don't need to go into them here. Suffice to say, the most striking thing about his story is when he got in trouble, no one spoke up to defend him. Long before his behavior became public knowledge, he must have treated enough people poorly that it came back to haunt him.

My guess is if Meryl Streep did something wrong and the public got wind of it, others would rise up to defend her. She'd get a pass.

In turn, I hope if I ever do anything wrong, people will stand up for me too, because I've tried to live my life properly and with integrity.

You have to live a disciplined life to become respected, and you have to respect others. Another rabbi friend of mine embodies this well. He knows I'm not the most religious guy, but he's so accepting of me that I am compelled to be the same way toward him. "Glenn," he says, "I know you lead a good life, and I respect you for that. I don't expect you to live the life that I did."

Ultimately, the point is that you need to learn from others if you're going win your race against failure. You don't have to *be* them, and you certainly don't have to live the life they lead, but if you are disciplined, you will find you can learn from anyone.

THE DIFFERENCE BETWEEN LUCK AND SKILL

The disciplined person is going to see more opportunities in life than the person sitting in front of the TV waiting for their ship to arrive. In other words, if you hold yourself to your goals and work hard, you create your own luck.

This is the value of waking up earlier, working harder, learning from everything, and putting yourself in front of the right people. Through the sheer volume of your activity, your fortunes will improve.

In real estate, I see two kinds of brokers. Some are creative, constantly looking for new ways to create business. They don't wait for the phone to ring; they go out and find their next sale. Others put up a sale sign, maybe place an ad or two, and wait to see what happens.

By now, you know what kind of person I am and which camp I fall into. I didn't wait for the phone to ring. I *made* the phone ring.

When I was young, I put fliers on windshields for my parents' business until we generated new leads. When I delivered papers, I knocked on every door I saw and asked everyone if they would like a paper delivered to their door.

I couldn't believe how many new customers I would get by taking the time to ask. This meant more money from the subscriptions and also more money from the tips. Like interest, opportunity has a way of compounding itself.

Sometimes, those opportunities don't manifest until years later. One of my customers bought newspapers from me for four or five years. She loved me and my commitment to my paper route. Every Friday when it came time to collect, I learned quickly she was also one of my best tippers. I'm sure part of this was because I was her son's friend, but I know the rest is because I did a good job.

About a decade later, I had traded in the newspaper route for my father's business. I began as the only salesman, but as the company grew, I built an entire sales team to support me and realized I needed a director of marketing.

As it worked out, I hired my old customer, my best tipper, to fill the position, and she became an indispensable part of our business.

I like to think there's a certain connectivity in doing the right thing. Ten years before, we developed a mutual respect for each other. She did the right things back then, and when the opportunity arose, I did the right thing by her.

The disciplined person, especially the disciplined person who lives up to their own values, leaves a lasting impression on others. They will remember you for the work you did and the value you created. You never know how that's going to pay off down the road, but trust me: it will.

CAREGIVERS ON CALL: CREATING OUR OWN LUCK

In 1990, we started a company called Caregivers on Call. The idea of work-life balance was taking off at the time, a concept companies like Google and Apple would champion later in the decade, and I wanted to build a family-friendly company that reflected those ideals.

In many ways, this idea was nothing new to us. My parents believed there was a correlation between happiness at home and success in business. Today, research bears this out.

Because of this, we found ourselves in a good position when the work-life balance idea caught on. We understood what it was all about, and we knew how to develop the market. At first, we set up Caregivers on Call to help employees at other companies who needed childcare when their normal arrangements fell through, but eventually we assisted with a multitude of employee needs.

Viacom signed on as our first client, but only after a marathon seventeen-hour phone call to hash out all the details of our contract. We started at seven o'clock one morning and finished at two o'clock the next. To this day, I can safely say there is no kind of discipline quite like sitting through a call of that length.

Within about four hours of the call ending, we had a qualified, vetted caregiver at the home of a Viacom employee who couldn't find childcare elsewhere.

The service became an immediate hit, and Viacom decided they needed to scale the program to employees all across the country. At the same time, we offered services to other big companies like KPMG, Time Warner, and countless law firms.

Because we enabled employees to get work done, every company found that our service more than paid for itself. This was especially true for the law firms, as it created more billable hours for their lawyers.

At the same time, I was still running our home-care business and a number of other start-ups at our family company. Between the companies, we all worked like dogs, first to roll out this new service, and then quickly to scale it to meet demand.

In this way, we created our own luck. We took care to watch business trends and identify a need. We worked literally night and day to build out the service to assure clients of our integrity. Finally, we put in the time and mileage to maintain a quality, respectable service as the company took off.

You could say we were lucky to cash in on a trend, but make no mistake: we never would have had the opportunity in the first place if not for a disciplined approach.

Eventually, Caregivers on Call was recognized as one of the nation's most family-friendly companies during a ceremony at the White House Rose Garden, and I even got to meet Bill and Hillary Clinton. It was all a tremendous honor, though I felt like small potatoes standing next to high rollers like the CEO of Citibank and other leaders of Fortune 500 companies.

With Caregivers on Call, we saw the inner workings of certain companies whose leadership lacked basic discipline, who adopted programs and policies, not because it was worth doing, but because it would make them look good in front of their shareholders. I was shocked the first time I heard a company tell me they wanted Caregivers on Call purely so they could mention us in the employee handbook, and they had no intention of pursuing the program beyond that.

In truth, I shouldn't have been too surprised. The whole corporate culture there was "eat what you kill." They knew incoming employees cared about work-life balance, and so they wanted to appear family-friendly—but they weren't.

When the world markets collapsed nearly a decade later, nobody came to bail them out. Everybody knew their reputation, and nobody missed them after they went belly-up.

Even something like culture comes down to discipline. You can pay lip service to something all you want, but until you put in the daily effort to create results and stand for what you say you do, whatever you put down in the employee manual won't amount to much.

No one wants to feel as if they're just filling space to help make a profit. From the beginning, commit to training your employees and doing things the right way, and renew that commitment constantly. Discipline is nothing if not a long-term investment.

BEING STRONG WITHOUT BEING STUBBORN

In my own family, I've seen this investment pay off tenfold. Now the president of two different companies, Jordan embodies the disciplined life. He's the first to arrive to the office and the last to leave. Yet somehow, he still manages to absorb countless books on leadership and maintain his passion for Brazilian jiu-jitsu.

For my part, I work tirelessly to mentor and train everyone willing to listen, whether it's Jordan, my other children, or the senior leadership at our companies. Over the years, I've made it a point to model a philosophy of doing things the right way, which I hope is reflected in how we treat our vendors, customers, and employees.

I've learned that however much I give, I get more back in return. Others may not realize it, but my mentorship has been a two-way street. I learn constantly from those around me, and through them, I learn how to be a better leader.

Often, watching others helps you learn how to reach your goals in different ways. At all of my companies, any time a salesperson and a customer aren't getting through to each other, if they're butting heads to no end, we encourage the salesperson to pass the customer off.

Naturally, this is tough for a lot of people, who feel as if they've been forced to give up. I've never seen it that way. If you realize you're not getting through to someone but you know someone else can, then you've just saved a sale and helped your company out in the process. It's just a different method to achieve success.

Because we put so much care into training our employees in doing things the right way, this rarely happens. When it does, however, we make sure they understand everyone is better off for it.

Part of being disciplined is learning to get things done more effectively and efficiently without cutting corners. This doesn't happen overnight, but if you commit to adapting, you can certainly accelerate the process.

The more you put yourself out there, the more you will

take in. Understanding this is the easy part. The biggest question is *whether* you're willing to do it, and for how long. Once you've tasted success, will you ease back and let yourself coast? Or will you renew your efforts, set new targets, and learn to become even more effective?

IN BUSINESS, FIRST WINS

Any industry is segmented by things like size, product, and location. Wherever you and your competitors fall within that, one thing is certain: only the top few companies will survive.

Mixology exists in a narrowly defined area of contemporary fashion. In our region, we have roughly twenty competitors. Eventually, sixteen or seventeen of them will hang up their jackets and call it quits.

This is nothing against any of these businesses. However, in the race against failure, most ventures can no longer keep pace after about five years. It may be a harsh truth, but if your goal isn't to rank among the best in your industry, you're probably not going to make it.

Patterns like this exist at the employee level as well, where you have your A, B, and C players. Every team only has a couple of spots for the A players, and only the overachievers get there consistently.

Making the A squad takes a commitment of mind, body, and soul. It takes a daily strategy to get there, and it requires a particular kind of discipline to carry that out.

If you're not on the A team yet, take the initiative to figure out why. Are you satisfied where you are, in fifth place or lower, or are you still learning how to put the pieces all together to become more effective at your job?

Discipline is repetition. The grind isn't glamorous, but it can bring glory. The person who starts their day at 6:30, exercises, and sits down to work by 7:30 is going to have an advantage over the slow riser who spends their first few hours reading the news and getting comfortable before getting to work around eleven o'clock.

I feel strongly about how people should get started with their workday, but after that, the rest is up to them.

I don't want to hire anyone I must supervise. Naturally, every company has rules to follow, but otherwise I encourage my employees to be independent and creative.

For instance, the director of web content at Mixology began as a salesperson in one of our stores. When it became clear that her talents extended well beyond sales, we gave her more responsibility and the freedom to make the position her own.

Since then, our web presence has grown tremendously under her leadership. We invested in her and her creativity, and we couldn't be happier with the results.

Discipline is not the same as boxing people in. My entire career, I've looked for the brightest, most creative minds and encouraged them to chart their own paths.

I call this human credit. Sure, we pay the people we invest in, but the real investment is in their minds, their creativity, and even their happiness. When you're engaged around your work, you can't wait to be there and bring every ounce of your personality to bear on a project. In that kind of situation, the discipline part comes easy.

A lot of business leaders say they give their employees enough rope to hang themselves. Not me. I'm looking for the next leaders to mentor, not the next person to fire.

I give all my employees the freedom to innovate, build, and develop. If they have potential but need more training or education to get there, I'll make it happen.

Teaching others discipline comes from setting goals for them and having faith in their ability to execute them. Good leaders don't need to micromanage the process.

Just share your goal, explain your reasoning, and trust they'll make you proud.

JOE PRASAD AND THE DISCIPLINED LIFE

Joe Prasad is a man of great experience. I like to say his stories have stories, and I'm fortunate he and I have shared so many of them together over the years.

Joe came to America from Fiji when he was fifteen, finished high school, and set out on his own in a foreign country. Soon, he managed to find a job at a bar and grill and put himself through college.

By twenty, he had finished school and worked for my father and me. He began as a gofer and quickly worked his way up.

I'll let Joe explain his time with us together in his own words in a moment, but for now, I'll say he didn't peak when he worked for us. After we sold our business, his star kept rising and never stopped.

I told Joe that one day he'd be president of a Fortune 500 or 1,000 company. After working for some time as the sales manager for LifeLine's government business division, these days he's running a division for Medtronic, the medical equipment company. Still, I wouldn't be surprised to find him in the C-Suite down the road. The rest of the story, I'll leave up to Joe.

· · · · ·

It's hard to imagine it was twenty-six years ago that I walked into Plaza Nurses Agency office building. I met Glenn's father for my interview in his seven-by-twelve office, and though he hired me immediately, I requested a start date of March 11, so I could give notice at my part-time college job. What was I even thinking?

Little did I realize this fateful encounter with the senior Edwards would be life-changing. How fortunate was I to have met such a wonderful family man and the owner of a very successful home health-care business? I was fresh out of St. Johns University with a degree in finance. Having only arrived to New York four years ago from the Fiji Islands, I had big aspirations. Graduating in January 1991, in the midst of a significant recession and with the backdrop of a Middle East conflict in Iraq, I had slim pickings as a new graduate.

At the start of my first day, I arrived promptly at 8:30 a.m. Moments later, a tall man with curly hair walked out and introduced himself to me.

"Hi, I am Glenn Edwards, and starting today, you will be Joe!"

I kid you not, those were Glenn's first words to me. Frankly, I did not care at this point, as people had always struggled with my first name. I wanted to get to work and earn a paycheck! For the record, to this day I am still Joe in all my professional dealings.

I had much to learn. There was no such thing as home health care in Fiji, let alone personal emergency response systems. Spending four years in New York while going to college exposed me to a new way of life, but there was still so much more I didn't know.

Working for the Edwards family was a truly humbling experience. Every day, we helped families manage crises with their loved ones, since no one can ever adequately prepare for the day when they might have to take care of an ailing family member. In our open office, phones rang all over the place as employees scrambled to help the countless families in need.

Glenn was always on the front lines talking to families and setting them up with someone to help care for their sick family members. He was the most talented employee there. He had an amazing ability to calm whoever was calling and assure them we could help. It was rare that a first-time caller chose not to do business with us. Not only would he speak with the new customer, but he would also inevitably find the most amazing caregiver to go work for them.

As time went on, I got to know Glenn very well and enjoyed the mentoring sessions he would provide. He took an interest in helping me, which I saw as genuine. He took an interest in helping me learn the business, but also went on to advise me on many aspects of life and living in the United States. Whether it was politics or investing, he had an angle to share that I had not yet considered.

I'll never forget the time he shared his thoughts with me on Bernie Williams's demands for a new contract with the Yankees. Of course, at the time I was trying to negotiate a salary increase for myself. He told me just because Bernie believed he was worth $12 million did not mean he should automatically get it. He reminded me that the value of that increase would be short-lived compared to how Bernie felt about his job, all things considered. Money wasn't everything. I was young at the time and couldn't understand how Bernie's situation applied to mine, but let's say that was the last time we negotiated a salary increase.

When Glenn had an idea for a new business, I decided to follow him. Despite a three-year ramp-up and with minimal resources, we realized we had stumbled upon something truly big. He gave me tremendous leeway to consider how we might sustain our success.

We negotiated many contracts together, none bigger than the contract he signed in December 1996. Working closely together, we had successfully negotiated a long-term deal that would give us access to market-leading technology. It was a home run for all involved.

I remember how grateful I was to be working for such a patient family. Glenn did not strike me as a get-rich-quick kind of guy, although he would frequently walk by my desk to see how many orders we had taken that day. While I was super excited to share the good numbers, I was surprised to find he never looked disappointed when the numbers were poor. He managed to find the most encouraging advice for me.

Honestly, as much as I wanted to feel I was a special employee for this tiny business, I also felt he had the same words of encouragement and giving way for any of his employees. He genuinely took an interest in everyone, showing he truly believed money wasn't everything!

To this day, I reflect on all the good times working for Glenn and his family. It has served me well. I learned about family, families in crisis, patience, golf, skiing, appreciating all the good things in life, and empathy. How fortunate was this young man from Fiji?

EXERCISE: WHAT DOES DISCIPLINE MEAN TO YOU?

The race against failure is a marathon, not a sprint. While all good leaders know to begin with the end in mind, no two people are going to train the same way to get there. Use the space below to answer the following questions.

1. How do you use discipline to serve your own best interests?

2. What does your daily routine look like? Is it helping you achieve your goals, or does it need adjusting?

3. To you, what is the difference, if any, between discipline in your personal and professional lives?

4. How can you maintain discipline in both your personal and professional lives without neglecting one or the other?

DISCIPLINE MEANS HAVING SKIN IN THE GAME

Good leaders know not only how to get the best out of themselves, but also how to get the best out of others. This lies at the center of competition and collaboration, which we'll explore in the next chapter.

Of course, delegation isn't an excuse to relax and let other people do the heavy lifting. Senior leaders in the most successful businesses often ping-pong between so many duties it can make your head spin just to watch them. However, there is only so much any reasonable person can be expected to do.

One of my favorite examples of this comes from the 1980s, when Chrysler was in danger of going out of business. The senior management team had impeccable automotive credentials and knew their business incredibly well, yet no one could figure out why the company was failing.

Eventually, it came to light that none of them had any frontline responsibilities. They may have had some great minds at the top, but they weren't applying them to the reality of the workplace.

Quickly, they pivoted, putting each senior manager directly in charge of a different department within the company. Soon, things turned around.

The lesson isn't hard to grasp: it's one thing to delegate certain responsibilities to capable hands. However, it's another thing entirely not to have any skin in the game.

The best businesses have their best people on the front lines. Not only does it build accountability with your employees, but it also builds a far greater understanding of what is actually going on in your company.

CHAPTER FIVE

The Power of Competition and Collaboration

· · · · ·

When I look at New England Patriots coach Bill Belichick managing from the sidelines, I see a lot to admire in the way he collaborates with his players and fellow coaches in the face of competition.

This was especially apparent in the 2017 Super Bowl, one of the greatest comebacks in the history of the sport. If you watched Belichik from the sidelines, you couldn't tell if his team was winning or losing. He had complete faith in his offensive and defensive coordinators, as well as in everyone else on his senior management team.

As the head coach, Belichick sets the vision and trains his team on how to implement it. He trusts them to put this vision into action, and they do. When you watch the Patriots, you can see they have a clear strategy going into every game. No matter how things are going, Bill Belichick doesn't run up and down the sidelines screaming at people, because he has no reason to. He knows his team is prepared.

The best competitors are prepared and rely on the talents of their teams to execute their plans. The game never speeds up on them; they're always in control. If the Patriots end up down a few points, they identify where they're not executing, revise their plan, and set back out to win.

THE VALUE OF THE UNQUANTIFIABLE

The value of preparation in the face of competition isn't always quantifiable. However, we can always identify new signposts of success.

In sports, the most obvious measure is the win-loss record. This is a great indicator of organizational success, but the best organizations probe far deeper. What's your win-loss record over both the short term and the long term? What do the differences or similarities tell you?

So much of this comes from the human side of things. Do you have many long-term employees? Do they speak highly of you? Are they productive, and do they get along with each other?

Taking things further, what's the state of your senior management team? Are they loyal, or are they looking for a way out? If they do leave, are they making a lateral move, or are they being promoted? If the latter, this actually reflects well on your organization, since it indicates that you've trained your team well and their skills are in demand.

How about your customers? When they visit, are your stores clean or dirty? Do your customers speak highly of you when given the opportunity? Does your brand inspire fans?

Looking at the Patriots again, they have some of the most diehard fans in all of football. This doesn't just come from having good players on the field. It comes from having a good team of collaborators in place throughout the organization. Senior management praises the coaching staff, the coaches praise ownership, the players praise the coaches, and the fans praise their players. It's almost a perfect example of how to run a business.

Looking over at baseball, the book and movie *Moneyball* explored other ways organizations could try to quantify the unquantifiable. The general manager of the Oakland Athletics, Billy Beane, and his team are largely credited with being the first baseball team to look at quantitative analytics to project outcomes over the season.

Whenever it comes to data, the real trick is how you use it and apply it. One thing the Athletics did, for instance, was look at how often a player would outperform their projections. They would ask how often a given team ends up in close games and look for other indicators that the team doesn't roll over and die.

With these metrics, they would then ask what kinds of things help an individual or group do better than they're expected to, and how that can be harnessed. They knew this kind of consistent outperformance could be at least partially attributed to a strong coaching staff, but what did that mean, and how could it be reproduced?

Billy Beane put his whole career on the line for taking this strategy with the Athletics. It required considerable buy-in from the rest of his staff, which was not immediately forthcoming. Baseball, like any sport, is a game of tradition, and Beane had to win out against a culture that preferred gut reactions and hunches over quantitative data.

Certainly, there is a place for gut reactions and hunches, but wouldn't any business want some data to bear those hunches out? We learned all about this push and pull in the early days of Mixology. We began as a by-the-gut company, and truly our founder who pushed this vision had great instincts, but we didn't find our footing until we brought data in to help guide and support our decisions.

In this way, your greatest competition is going to be within your own organization. If you are able to collaborate and bring a variety of skills and disciplines to bear, you are far more likely to succeed in the marketplace than if one person calls the shots and doesn't listen to others' opinions.

To me, the businesses that learn how to survive are the ones that figure out how to strike this balance. When you're first getting started, it doesn't matter what the outside world is doing. Focus on survival strategies like working together and nurturing the things that already make you successful.

What your competition is doing certainly matters, especially in the long term, but the road to becoming best in class begins with what you're doing within your own walls.

The more specific you get, the better. Don't just strive to be the best in a general sense. Be the best in organizational strategies, in buying strategies, in selling strategies. Become the best in enough of these metrics, and you will become the best overall.

No leader accomplishes this without absolute trust in their team. Again, sports analytics have demonstrated the value of this trust in revealing ways. Recently, I watched a segment on the Brooklyn Nets' fan-favorite player Jeremy Lin, who trains with one of the largest analytics-based firms in the world. Their philosophy is based on the old adage "work smarter, not harder," but emerging technology and thinking have allowed them to approach this goal in exciting new ways.

In a nutshell, this firm monitors athletes to determine the amount of physical stress they take during practice. Once an athlete like Lin has reached a predetermined point, they'll take the player off the court and tell them they're done for the day.

Certainly, this goes against the common wisdom, which states the more players practice, the better they'll get. However, sports scientists have learned that continued practice brings diminishing returns. At a certain point, players can do more harm for themselves than good.

Whether you're an athlete or a business leader, it takes a certain kind of mindset to trust recommendations that may go against common practice. However, if you surround yourself with people you trust and who have proven track records, your faith in them is more likely to pay off than not.

When I said in chapter 4 that I'm constantly listening and learning, even from those I mentor, this is what I mean. The advanced analytics side of business wasn't necessarily available to me as I made my career. It is now, however, and I've watched Jordan apply it at Mixology to tremendous results.

That said, he'll be the first to tell you neither he nor his approach is perfect. However, he works constantly to challenge his own understanding of how to run a business. More importantly, he builds teams that share this mindset: don't worry about being perfect, but work to improve your approach every day.

HOW COMPETITION AND COLLABORATION INTERSECT

In my experience, when one of your competitors first sets up shop, sometimes literally opening up next door, across the street, or in the same shopping center as you, many within your organization will be ready to hit the panic button.

I've seen managers freak out over a competitor's lower prices and accuse landlords of foul play by leasing space to one of our rivals. I've seen the responses play out in a lot of different ways, and my own response has been the same: calm down.

The mantra in any of my businesses has been "we do what we do." We follow our own strategies, and we embrace our competition. Watch what they're doing and learn from them if you can, but don't freak out, and don't run. Just be better.

Competition won't kill you if you embrace it. Stay on your own game, focus on the three Ps—product, process, and personnel—and you'll do just fine.

When one of Mixology's direct competitors moved in near us, we focused on what we did best and redoubled our efforts. Soon, with our same management team and in the same retail space, our sales grew by 40 percent.

Things could have gone much differently, and they almost did. At first, some on the management team were belligerent. They wanted to confront the landlord and tell him what a horrible person he was for doing this to us.

I pushed back, saying all the fighting in the world wouldn't change the reality of the situation. First, we didn't have a right to exclusivity in the shopping center. Further, when we moved in, the competition that was already there probably felt the same way about us.

If you're good at what you do, whatever your competition does is irrelevant to your business.

You can throw your hands in the air and dream of doomsday scenarios for your business all you like. However, every time you do that, you're failing to recognize the opportunity in the moment.

In our case, it was important to think about how shopping centers work. People like variety. Two or three competing stores are a better draw than one. If there are more options, people will come from farther away, because they appreciate the selection. All we had to do was give people a reason to come to our stores and shop with us.

Eventually, after our sales surged, everyone from management down became believers. You can't stop your competition. You can't tell them not to open. In fact, you want to see your competition open new stores. If they're not, it probably means people aren't shopping. If they're not shopping, you'll eventually be out of business anyway.

I've been around long enough and worked in enough industries to know the story is the same in any era. Just the names change. I've heard people say Amazon, Macy's, or Bloomingdales will put them out of business.

In my experience, the only one that can put you out of business is yourself.

WHEN COMPETITION GETS UGLY

While a student at Northeastern University, my daughter, Gabrielle, interned as a floater at Saks Fifth Avenue, a prominent New York department store with a great legacy. She worked in different departments throughout the store, usually for about two or three weeks at a time.

Partly because she already had considerable retail experience and partly because they didn't have much in the way of formal training programs, management essentially threw her on the sales floor and let her learn for herself.

Gabrielle is a lot like me. She doesn't just like selling; she likes selling *more*. Her work at Saks Fifth Avenue drove her sense of accomplishment, boosted her commission, and made an otherwise shy person a force of nature whenever she was on the sales floor.

Every morning, they announced the top three salespeople of the previous day, and nearly every morning, my daughter ranked among them. Whether she was selling handbags or formal wear, Gabrielle moved product.

Eventually, they put her in the men's department, where one day, she made a very big sale to a gentleman who shopped there regularly.

When the regular salesperson in the men's department heard about it, he intercepted the order and claimed it as his own. "I've been working here for twenty years," the salesman said. "You don't sell to my customer."

Gabrielle held her ground. "He walked in the store. I asked if I could help him, he came right over to me, and we went shopping."

At the time, my daughter thought that was the end of it, but in a toxic, winner-take-all work environment, the end is never the end. A couple days later, HR called Gabrielle to their office, told her the other salesperson had complained about her, and she was going to lose her job.

Not knowing what she did wrong, she called me for advice. "Daddy, how can they do this to me?" she asked.

"You did nothing wrong," I said. "I've hired thousands of people. They can't discharge you for selling too many goods. They can only discharge you for cause. Go back up to the office, walk into the HR department, and demand they provide a reason for discharging you."

Ultimately, standing up for herself worked. The management at Saks Fifth Avenue kept Gabrielle on and transferred her to another department. After her internship ended, they offered her a permanent position, which she declined to work for Mixology.

When I speak to the value of competition, this story shows the antithesis of my own views. Gabrielle learned firsthand what a culture built around nepotism and self-preservation can be like, and it isn't pretty.

Saks has great products. In fact, both my wife and my daughter shop there. However, their culture remains sorely lacking. The salespeople are miserable, and it's no surprise why. A workplace built around infighting and brinkmanship will not do as well as one built around customers and internal collaboration.

These days, Gabrielle is our head buyer at Mixology. She has helped us open stores in Manhattan, Scarsdale, and Rye, which have grown to become some of our flagship stores.

She remains active at all these outlets, stopping in about three times a week to supervise others on the buying team and make herself available to her managers and staff. Taking another page out of the Edwards family playbook, she never micromanages anyone. She'll give advice and step in where needed, but otherwise she affords her teams a great deal of autonomy.

HOW TO CREATE HEALTHY COMPETITION

I often say there's nothing wrong with arguing if your goal is to get better. Toxic infighting may be no good, but neither is going along to get along.

At my companies, we argue to get better. We're not jockeying for positions or trying to undercut our coworkers. Instead, we each have different ideas for how to move the company forward, and sometimes those ideas come from conflict.

If you can create an environment where leaders can argue passionately for their vision without things getting petty or personal, then you'll be doing your company a great service. You'd rather have that than an entire senior management team content with following the status quo.

During the George Steinbrenner years, the New York Yankees were a good example of this. Love him or hate him, Steinbrenner had a way of getting his staff and team to perform. They didn't always see eye-to-eye, but their shared commitment to the Yankees organization consistently came first.

The recently retired Derek Jeter played many of his best years under Steinbrenner. In fact, one of his best years came after Steinbrenner accused him of not working hard enough during the off-season. Not only did the Yankees go on to win a championship that year, but Jeter elevated his game to previously unseen levels.

The point is, if it's in service of the organization, if the bonds that hold the key players together are stronger than personal gain, then a little disagreement and strategic antagonizing is fine.

Similarly, a little competition never hurt anyone either. The managers at our Mixology stores compete with each other to see who gets the highest numbers on any given day. The difference between our managers and the salespeople at Saks Fifth Avenue, however, is they compete for fun and to better the company. Any personal reward is simply a by-product of the good work they do.

Mixology encourages this friendly competition, and to achieve it, we're transparent with our employees. Our managers know exactly what our other managers are doing, including who they sold to and how many units they sold.

Our philosophy is the more we give managers access to information, the better equipped they are to succeed. They're not required to use the information, but we find they do more often than not, as the friendly competition between stores constantly motivates them to step up their game.

COMPETITION BREEDS INNOVATION

The summer of my sixteenth birthday, I took a job cooking at my local KFC. At the time, at least in our restaurant, the food wasn't made fresh. Around four o'clock, in preparation for the dinner rush, the store lead would drop endless pieces of chickens into the deep fryers. By five, he'd be done, and we'd have more than enough chicken to get us through the night.

Even as a teenager, I could see this wasn't an ideal system. First, the customers were getting chicken that was often two or three hours old. Second, after making the chicken, my supervisor would waste his time the rest of the shift until it was time to close. It wasn't like he didn't have the free time to cook chicken in smaller batches throughout the shift.

Worst of all, however, was the amount of waste this produced. Depending on how busy it was, we'd usually have to throw away between 800 and 1,100 pieces of chicken.

Watching this every night drove me crazy. When my supervisor eventually left (most people don't last very long in fast food), I was put in charge of making the chicken.

Immediately, I resolved to cook the food in small batches based on demand. My goal was to sell all of the chicken we made every night. Usually, after accounting for bad pieces and other small hiccups, I only wasted between twelve and fifteen pieces.

Flash forward a few weeks. I was hard at work on an August afternoon when a limousine pulled up outside our restaurant. A few men in suits stepped out, walked in through the back, and said, "Can we speak with Glenn Edwards?"

I was afraid I'd done something wrong at this point, but I spoke up all the same: "I'm Glenn Edwards."

"We want to talk to you about the chicken over here," one of them said. "This is Mr. Solomon. He owns twenty-five KFC franchises, including this one, and he wants to know what you're doing."

"What do you mean?" I asked, still unsure what this was all about.

"We're accustomed to having tremendous waste at the end of the night, and we want to know how you're doing it."

Without throwing my previous manager under the bus, I explained my process. I told them we only tried to work ahead by about two or three orders to keep the food fresh and have as little leftover as possible.

"You're the only one in the franchise who does it this way," he said.

I said I didn't understand why, since my approach was so simple. They took their leave of me, and as far as I knew, that was that.

About a month later, I found out they wanted to put me in the manager training program. With school coming up and the tennis season calling my name, I politely declined and gave notice I was leaving. They even called my parents and begged them to convince me to stay on, but with all respect to the company, I was never destined to be a KFC lifer.

The lessons I got from KFC stuck with me. First, compete against yourself. If you know you can do better than whatever is expected of you, do it. Someone will notice. Second, compete against others if you aren't undermining anyone to do it. I helped that particular KFC become one of the most profitable of Mr. Solomon's twenty-five franchises, but I didn't get anyone in trouble to do it.

Finally, I learned how valuable talented people are—and how far managers will go to retain them. It felt good to be wanted as a teen, and so now I make sure all my own talent at my companies know how appreciated they are. When I look around Mixology and see how many employees in our still-young company have been with us since they were in high school or college, it fills me with pride that not only we found good people, but those same good people saw value in us and chose to stick around.

BRAD WEISBORD ON THE VALUE OF COMPETITION

Earlier in the book, I brought up Brad Weisbord, the intrepid lacrosse player who had a plan for getting the best of his opponents. These days, Brad enjoys a successful career buying and raising championship racehorses. While he's still got plenty of career left to go, he's already accomplished quite a bit in a short amount of time, learning a thing or two about leadership in the face of competition.

At its essence, his philosophy is simple. "The best way to capitalize on the competition comes back to belief in yourself," Brad said. In his work, raising the best horses can lead to a lot of second-guessing, especially when trying out unproven methods: "Many times, I've found myself saying, 'I hope I'm not crazy doing this.'" Fortunately, more often than not, when he brings a new horse to market, his competitors are eager to learn about his new approach.

Brad may have proven he's built his success on a sound strategy rather than luck, but his age has remained a persistent sticking point for many prospective buyers. "I started in this business at twenty-one," Brad said, "but the average age of bloodstock agents and managers is fifty. People looked at me like I couldn't get a job in finance or real estate, so I came to disrupt their world."

The truth, of course, was far simpler. Brad had long been fascinated by the industry and saw an opportunity for himself he couldn't pass up. Brad had no interest in rocking the boat, but convincing others of this would take some work.

"It took great communication, market knowledge, analytical skills, and brutal honesty to overcome this challenge."

As a young business leader himself, Brad has plenty of advice for other aspiring leaders looking to get a leg up on their competition. According to Brad, it begins with passion. "I don't look at my job as work. I look at it as a hobby."

Next, aspiring leaders should practice patience. "Many young people look at the first deal and wonder how much is in it for them," Brad said. "In my first deal, I was just happy to be at the big boy's table working with the owner on the other side of the transaction. I knew he would see my worth." To illustrate his point, Brad said, while he may not have made too much in his first ten deals, his most recent deals have brought in at least ten times as much.

Everyone makes mistakes or loses ground to their competitors from time to time, Brad said, but a dedicated leader can come back from just about anything. To him, the trick to staying competitive is simple. "Your word is our bond. Once you can't be trusted, you will have to find something else to do."

EXERCISE: HOW DOES COMPETITION AND COLLABORATION MAKE YOU BETTER?

Competition motivates each of us a little differently, but it can drive just about any of us to new heights. Use the space below to answer the following questions.

1. How do you face competition?

2. What do you do well, and what do you need to work on? In either case, why? How can you improve?

3. How do you collaborate with others? Describe what you bring to the table in collaborative environments.

4. Do you have any allies in your organization? How do you bring out the best in each other?

SAFETY IN NUMBERS

The nice thing about having competition is you have a proven marketplace. In such a situation, all you have to do is learn where your competitors are vulnerable and build a service that does things better.

This is exactly what we did when we expanded our home-care business in Florida. To test out the market, we waited until five o'clock in the evening and called the local home-care agencies to see if they could provide a live-in nurse's aide that evening. Many of them couldn't. Immediately, we knew what our point of difference would be.

Competition like this happens all the time. We know our competitors shop at Mixology and walk the floor to see how we're set up. Sometimes, they'll order things online and then send it back to see how we respond. I don't see anything wrong with it. Better to embrace your competition and understand what they're doing than try to fight them.

In this way, competition can be extremely valuable, which is why I maintain good relationships with my competitors. After all, you never know when, or how, it could help you.

Sometimes, not having any competition can make your work more difficult. When we first started Caregivers on

Call, nobody understood what we were about, and we ended up getting a lot more blank stares than sales.

Being first to market doesn't mean much if the market doesn't understand your product. You could have the best idea in the world, but if the world doesn't get it, then it doesn't matter.

While we ultimately found a great deal of success, Caregivers on Call was very challenging, very expensive, and very unfruitful up front. I had set the business up in a way that gave us plenty of time to find our footing, but I almost pulled the plug several times. We nearly failed, but our resilience got us through. I still look at this time as the greatest challenge of my career.

As we move on to the next chapter, I'll say this: eventually in business, you're going to come across challenges that seem insurmountable. In these moments, it's good to remember that you don't have to be an innovator. Sometimes, it's better to look around, remind yourself what works, and throw yourself back into the game.

Saying you're committed to success is one of the hardest commitments you will ever make. Resilience is a process of renewal, and if you're going to stick your neck out as an entrepreneur, it's essential to see it through. Be committed all the way!

CHAPTER SIX

The Power of Failure and Resilience

· · · · ·

When you're competing in sports, there's a fine line between insecurity and total confidence. Business is no different. In both, failure is always right behind you, and you have to run as fast as you can to succeed.

As a young athlete, I went into every competition thinking I was going to win. It didn't matter how skilled I or my team was, or how much better the opposition was in comparison. I figured I had a shot, even if it turned out we would lose in the end.

Sports teach us that, sometimes, being successful means only winning 51 percent of the time. You'll often hear coaches and athletes talk about the importance of having a short memory; even if you lose, it's up to you to pick yourself up and be ready to start over the next day.

Even the best teams lose. Even the best businessmen lose. However, the best ones get right back up to do it all again.

If you approach your career knowing you're going to lose sometimes, the next step is learning how to pick your spots and squeeze out more wins.

Over the season, the best teams know how to look ahead on their schedule and project the games they *should* win and those they *must* win. Even when they know they're most likely going to lose, they work to perform to their fullest on the field.

Remember, a high probability of losing doesn't mean you *will* lose. Projections are one thing, but as they say, you've still got to play the game. In these scenarios, even if you do lose, you will get more out of it the more you learn and the more you put into it.

Win or lose, resilience means preparing yourself for each moment to the best of your abilities. After all, the great thing about resilience is it has a compounding affect: not only will you perform better for the big game, but you'll also perform better for the next game.

TAKE THE INTERVIEW—AND SHOW UP

I often say you should take every job interview that comes your way. It doesn't matter if you don't want the job. Interviewing takes practice like everything else. Think of it as training for your best interview, the one that will land you your dream job down the road.

Especially when you're starting out, it's easy to make excuses. Maybe you don't want to move. Maybe the hours stink. Maybe the salary isn't competitive. You can think of a million reasons not to take any job, but that's not the point.

With every interview, here's something to keep in mind: most of the places that call to interview you have little intention of hiring you. For any given job, they're looking at ten, fifteen, twenty people or more. When they meet you, they know you most likely won't get the job, but they interview you anyway, because they're looking for the best person.

My advice? Use them like they're using you. They're trying to cull a field of qualified candidates, and you're trying to build your interviewing skills for important interviews.

In reality, you're not just training to become a better interviewee. You're also learning resilience in the face of rejection. Most jobs you interview for you're not going to get. It stings, especially the first few times you go through it.

However, the less vulnerable to rejection you are, the more you'll learn—and the more you'll learn how to close. We're not often told this growing up, but even rejection is something we need to practice.

Whether it's sales, interviews, or anything else, there's a transition that takes place between the first time you stick your neck out and the tenth. If you're willing to pay attention to what's working and what isn't, you'll surprise yourself at how quickly you'll learn to turn an initial "no" into a "yes."

Every profession is going to have its superstars, its Michael Jordans, Tiger Woodses, and Mickey Mantles who are so naturally gifted that every door seems wide open for them. They're going to see success far more often than most people, but they still have to play every game.

The great thing about a good team is, regardless of talent, if everyone puts in the work, you're going to lift each other up to become something greater than the sum of your parts. Even then, it takes resilience to find everyone's best skills, train collaboratively, and set actionable goals.

Of course, first you've got to find a team. To do that, you have to get yourself in the game. Knock on every door, take every interview, and accept every rejection until you've found your way forward.

DON'T ACCEPT LIMITS TO WHAT YOU CAN DO

When I think of the power of resilience in the face of failure, my mind often turns to Stacey Griffith, one of the original instructors at SoulCycle. Griffith has become tremendously successful in an area where there was no real blueprint for success before her.

Historically, people have viewed personal trainers as affable gym rats, though perhaps not the most highly educated bunch. While this stereotype is certainly not the most flattering for those in the profession, it has persisted nevertheless.

Griffith took one look at this stereotype and said it wasn't for her. She specialized in the areas she taught, and, roughly in the middle of the 2000s, she worked with SoulCycle. Now, more than a decade later, the company continues to expand, setting up locations across the country.

These days, Griffith is a celebrity instructor/entrepreneur with a successful book promoted by Oprah. She saw an opportunity and built her brand centered around positivity and empowerment, and she persisted until she got where she wanted to be. As SoulCycle prepares to go public, Griffith's stake in the business is now worth many millions.

The difference between the Michael Jordans of a profession and everyone else is that these stars are visionaries. Griffith could have gone on running her spinning classes like the rest of the personal trainers in the country. She would have made a decent, if unremarkable, living for herself. However, she realized that so much of personal fitness had to do with culture and community, and so she built a unique brand and program centered around those goals.

Her classes are captivating. Both my wife and I have attended them for years, and there's never an empty seat in the room. If you take a moment and do the math, assuming about sixty or seventy people per class at about thirty to thirty-five dollars a head, you can understand why her business model has become so successful. A skilled trainer might gross a hundred dollars in a forty-five-minute session. Griffith is easily clearing between ten and twenty times that amount.

In fact, Griffith's SoulCycle brand has become so popular that she and the leaders on her team are fitness rock stars.

Some have even enjoyed modeling stints and screen time in national commercials and print ads.

The point is, Griffith could never have imagined the level of success she currently enjoys. However, she was resilient, tirelessly putting in the work to see how far this opportunity would take her.

So much success is built on this one element. Anyone willing to put in the time can see similar results, but so few actually do. We all say we know the value of resilience, but most don't practice it. Whenever I learn of a personal success story like Griffith's, my heart fills with admiration for that person's accomplishment.

GOOD IDEAS ARE GOOD IDEAS

I'm not perfect. I can think of plenty of things I'm not great at. In person, I'm usually quite humble about my skills and accomplishments—that is, unless it involves sales.

I know I'm a good salesman. I always have been. However, I also am smart enough to realize that, as good as I am at this one thing, this skill alone is not enough to run a successful business.

Do you want to know one of the best ways to avoid failure? Accept you can't go at it alone. No one is great at everything, but the best leaders know how to surround themselves with people who are great in complementary ways.

Even more, the best leaders create an environment where it's okay to fail. I encourage my employees to take chances. To whatever extent possible, I want them to feel like they control their own destiny. Especially at Mixology, where Jordan has taken my philosophy and run with it, we've created an environment where employees are throwing new ideas at us every day.

Not every single idea has to be a game changer to be valuable. Good ideas are good ideas, whether they revolutionize a brand or help simplify a day-to-day task.

For instance, recently one of our employees came up to me and Jordan and told us she'd met one of the greatest PR people in fashion she's ever seen and we should meet her. Another came up to us and suggested a few new advertising channels that looked like a good fit for our brand, but that we had so far overlooked. Especially in the age of viral marketing, where spontaneous creativity often packs more punch than strictly branded messages, we let our employees take plenty of risks with what they share from branch to branch.

People who don't take risks are missing out. When you take risks, when you stop playing it safe and start thinking outside the box, you're more engaged. You may risk more frequent failure, but you also increase your chances for greater success.

Besides, what's so bad about failure anyway? In sports, even the best teams only win about 70 to 80 percent of the time. In baseball, if you get three hits out of every ten at bats, they'll pay you $20 million a year and put you in the Hall of Fame.

Even if you're the best, failure is part of success. You might as well fail on your own terms.

With failure, your only questions should be these: how smart are you going to be, how are you going to learn from your mistakes, and how are you going to build on your successes? These are the questions resilient leaders ask themselves if they hope to build a sustainable business.

SNOW DAYS HAPPEN

Here's another leadership question: what do you do on a snow day, whether literal or metaphorical? Certainly, it's a chance to stop, relax, and smell the roses a little, but it's also a chance to take stock of your work and strategize for the coming weeks and months.

Depending on what business you're in, a snow day for everyone else can be an all-hands-on-deck effort for you. In New York, I've seen a few record snow days throughout my career. During one such event, the trains were shut down throughout the city, and the only way to get anywhere was by foot.

The workers at All Metro Health Care did exactly that. It goes without saying that health care doesn't take a break for a snowy day. We had patients to look after, and I was astounded to watch my nurse's aides put their patients before their families and brave the harsh winter weather—with some literally walking across the Brooklyn Bridge—so they could give our clients the assistance they needed.

Especially back then, health care wasn't exactly the highest-paying profession. Their commitment had nothing to do with money. It had to do with the drive, character, and concern for others that led them to this profession in the first place. In the face of immense challenges, they chose to do the right thing.

Even with the selfless work of these brave nurse's aides, snow days would still cost our company a fortune. However, I learned that things like this are a fact of life. These days, I use the concept of snow days to speak to any setback or unexpected event, because whatever business you're in, you're going to experience them.

Skilled leaders know these eventual setbacks have budgeting implications. When they do their modeling and projections, they factor a certain amount of these days in. Whether it's a snow day, an emergency repair, or an employee suddenly walking out on you, know it's going to happen, and it's going to cost you money.

Anticipating and preparing for snow days is one way to make a win from a seeming loss. Another is to make yourself useful on those days. Whatever happens, whether you lose your job or are actually snowed in, make it productive.

Maybe you need to catch up on sleep. There's nothing wrong with that; everyone needs to recharge. Maybe there's a task you haven't been able to get around to. Now's your chance. Maybe you need to take stock of your career, a current project, or some other pressing issue. Today is the day.

The point is, snow days don't have to be lost days. The most resilient leaders know how to seize on the opportunity of every moment, especially in the face of what others might consider a setback.

WISDOM FROM THE SCHOOL OF HARD KNOCKS

When Steve Tenedios was thirteen, he immigrated to the United States with his family and worked at his uncle's donut shop. Although he never went to college, he quickly climbed the business ladder in New York City, and today he has about 1,300 people working for him across roughly thirty restaurants in New York City.

In addition, this sophisticated businessman found even more success in his real-estate ventures, as well as other investments, along the way. If you're looking for a get-up-early, hardworking businessman, you'll find no greater mentor.

Steve believes every business leader must learn to recover from failure. "Being able to understand what you initially did wrong and what needs to be done differently is one of the many things that ultimately determines how far you will go in your field," he said. "If you see your mistakes, own them, and learn from them, then you're not going to make the same mistake again."

For Steve, this isn't just idle talk. Early in his career, he learned the value of treating his salespeople well in building a successful catering business. "I would hire them, train them, invest six to twelve months in them, paying them and helping them to grow their book of business," he said. Unfortunately, this up-front investment didn't always pay off. "More times than not, they would end up being poached for a few dollars more, taking their client list, and my business, with them."

The solution? Don't reinvent the wheel. Learn from the best practices of other industries. As Steve said, "I knew other types of businesses had restrictions on where their employees could work after leaving their jobs, but this wasn't heard of in the deli/catering business in the early eighties." After seeing far too many good employees get poached by competitors, Steve decided it was time the catering business had the same protections as other industries, so he had an attorney draft up a noncompeting contract. Afterward, his catering business started to see tremendous growth.

While Steve is a big believer in learning from failure, he would recommend putting in the work ahead of time to avoid it. As to what he considers the most valuable lesson he can impress upon young leaders, "Don't be afraid to fail. Be afraid of succeeding too soon. This could keep you from taking the chances needed to become a truly successful business leader."

In his many decades in business, Steve has learned enough life lessons to fill his own book. "My single most important lesson," Steve said, "is the ability to relate to others, to meet them at their level, and to empower them to treat your business like it is their business." Steve credits much of his success to this one lesson. "It transcends money and titles."

**EXERCISE: LEARNING RESILIENCE
IN THE FACE OF FAILURE**

I'm consistently amazed at how surprised people are when things go wrong. Sure, we all live for the high times, but if you let the highs get too high and the lows get too low, there's a good chance you're making things harder for yourself than they need to be. The good news is anyone can learn to anticipate failure and keep a level head in the moment. Use the space below to answer the following questions.

1. How have you failed? Think of a moment that particularly stands out for you, and describe it.

2. How did you react? How did you come to feel about it over time?

3. What did you learn? How did you apply that lesson to later situations?

4. What can you learn from failure? Identify three ways you can make failure a tool, rather than a crutch.

RESILIENCE IS INDISPENSABLE

It's important to commit to your work, remain resilient in the face of failure, and constantly search for opportunities to grow. It's equally important to work toward a full, balanced life that allows you to reach your full potential.

As we discussed earlier, this begins with a good work routine in which every day you get up, exercise, and try to be the first one to the office. After that, in the evenings or on the weekends, your time is yours to do with as you please.

I can say from experience, if you commit some of this time to giving back to your community—maybe through your church, synagogue, or other house of worship, or maybe through other channels—if you do it right and give back to a cause you're passionate about, the personal rewards can be immense.

If it's done for the right reasons, giving will make you a better person. It will make you better at your job or in your family life, because it inspires passion in you, and the great thing about passion is it carries into every aspect of your life.

In fact, today's leaders have become increasingly passionate about integrating a giving spirit into their business. I watched my parents embody this spirit as I grew up. At nighttime or on the weekends, my parents were incredibly active with their synagogue, their local Rotary chapter, and so many other organizations.

Even when my parents' business was small, my father made it a point to act as president for several professional associations. Once every few months, I'd watch all my parents' competitors gather in our living room and discuss pressing issues confronting their industry. My parents led these discussions, offering whatever resources they could to help their business community.

Competition aside, my parents understood that challenges affecting one of them impacted all of them. When we think about anticipation and resilience in the face of failure, never discount the power of community. In business and in life, I can think of no better lesson.

CHAPTER SEVEN

The Power of Charitable Motivations

· · · · ·

Through my parents, I learned that the makings of a charitable mindset begin at home.

I played Little League when I was about six or seven before moving on to basketball, tennis, and track in junior high and high school. My father rarely made it to a game, because he was working, but my mother made it to about every one.

Times have changed since then, and today's parents often have more flexible schedules than my parents did. It's great to see how many mothers and fathers are committed to making it out for all their kids' events as often as they do. It speaks to a genuine desire to be good and giving, and to take part in their communities.

That said, I advise people not to let their good intentions get the best of them. If they can afford to be at their children's games because their jobs or schedules allow it, then certainly they should. However, if they're struggling along at their work or experiencing financial difficulties, then perhaps the best way they can support their families is by staying away from the games and taking care of their professional lives.

I don't say this out of cruelty, especially not in a chapter about charitable motivations. However, cheering on your kids at the game is only one way of showing support. Having money, so they can buy equipment, is another.

I didn't hold it against my father that he couldn't make most of my games. He ran a one-man operation during a time when fathers were expected to be the sole breadwinners. I knew he cared, but I also knew his work was one of the most important things for our family's continued well-being.

When he did make it out, it was the last track meet of my senior year, and I was running the high hurdles. I'd won about every race that year and usually came in second or third when I didn't win. It had been a good year, and I wanted to cap it off right. The stakes were already high in my mind, but after learning my father would be there, I went into that final race more excited than I'd ever been.

I built a sizable lead quickly and was feeling good about myself. Then, I tripped over the last hurdle. Bloodied and with my opponents closing in on me, I dragged myself across the finish line to squeak out a win.

If this was the only time my father would ever see me run, at least I made it memorable.

My father may not have been able to make it out to my games, but I knew where he was—and I admired him for it. It wasn't like I missed my father. I grew up around the office, accompanying my dad to work during summers and on Saturdays.

Ultimately, he gave me plenty of his time, teaching me a great deal about work ethic, providing for your family, and giving back to the community however you can in the process.

BE THE FABRIC OF YOUR COMMUNITY—AND MEAN IT

I see charity or community work as a duty and a privilege,

not just something to make you competitive on your resume. In professions like teaching, giving back is a fundamental part of the work. In business, however, you often have to seek out opportunities to give back, because it's usually not a fundamental part of your job.

That said, I've noticed young professionals have a much greater awareness of community and charitable activities than I did in the early days of my career. I may have had the Kiwanis club at my school and taken part in social activities through that, but most other students didn't participate in such programs, because they weren't required to. Today, many high schools and colleges have clear community-service requirements that their students must fulfill.

Here's what I say to young leaders: if community service hasn't been required of you, require it of yourself. However, don't treat it like a chore. Find a way to give back that motivates you and makes you feel good about yourself. Whatever you choose to do, do it because you love it and genuinely want to help people.

Any company I've been a part of has established this spirit of giving as a core value. We love to find new ways to engage our community and help others at Mixology. Each of our stores hosts events for different causes throughout the year. For example, recently we collaborated with a band called Emergency Tiara during New York Fashion Week by producing a special run of T-shirts. We hosted an event, the band played, and all proceeds from the shirts went to a charity.

WATCH OUT FOR CHARITY LITE

It's good that many schools and organizations encourage students and employees to give back to their communities. That said, it should never feel like you're checking off a box, that you're going through the motions, only because it will help your career or make you a better person in some abstract way.

I call this mindset "charity lite." You may be helping out, but not for the right reasons. If your heart isn't in it, then what's the point?

Throughout this book, I talked about the importance of committing to what you do, to working hard at a job when everyone else might have called it a day.

My mindset for charitable work is no different. Don't just sign up for a club. Participate. Try to rise up in it and make a real contribution.

If you don't commit, then you don't get the emotional rewards. If you do commit, the payoff impacts all aspects of your life. For instance, maybe you came off a bad day at work but get a big lift from helping a kid learn to read while you're volunteering somewhere. That lift is going to make you feel a lot better about things when you show up to work the next day. Just a small bit of daily positivity can make the tough times a little easier.

Being charitable may be about giving to others, but it's the emotional payoff you get from it that will make it sustainable.

Giving a full-faced effort is like paying it forward. You get to stand alongside some great people and learn from them, and in turn they learn from you. Through this experience, you're better equipped to teach others how to give, or how to help, and they'll remember you for it.

I often tell people I'm not the expert on charitable giving. I learned from great people who showed me what to do, and now I'm trying to do the same for others.

If I've learned one thing in all of this, it's if I did more, I'd get more out of it. Every time I'm involved in a charitable program that speaks to me, I feel tremendous. Seek out that feeling in whatever charitable work you pursue.

PLAY TO YOUR STRENGTHS

Charitable work doesn't need to be completely divorced from your business. In fact, many of the charitable opportunities I pursue come directly out of my business ties. It's a natural by-product of the work I do, and it usually allows me to play to my strengths.

Back when I worked with Long Beach Hospital, our company did a lot of charitable work through them because they kindly asked us to get involved. Through our business relationship, they saw our particular talents and knew we could help them with certain programs.

On my end, the hospital recognized my skills as a salesperson and knew I would be an asset. As a result, I was named the chairman of their journal and put in charge of organizing the journal's dinner dance, one of their largest fundraising events.

With my success there, eventually they also put in me in charge of organizing their various golf outings, which took a lot of networking. Getting people to show up and spend money at a charity golf event takes a certain kind of tenacity. For every event, I had to call everybody I knew, as well as everybody that did business with the hospital. The work wasn't glamorous, but it was in my wheelhouse.

Much of my charity work has continued in this fashion. The gratitude, acceptance, and plaques that come with these events are all great, as is all the money we've been able to raise for good causes. For me, however, nothing beats that sense of a job well done, of looking out at all the friends, relatives, and business colleagues in the crowd and knowing they all showed up in part because of the work I put in.

Recently, I was able to bring everyone together for a fundraiser benefitting a children's hospital in Israel. Our goal was to raise enough money for an incubator for children born prematurely, which we did. In recognition of our efforts, the hospital even offered to send us an annual record of all the children it has helped. I look forward to watching this number grow as the years pass.

At the end of the day, I'm an entrepreneur. My business is real estate and clothing. However, the feeling I get from moments like these is enough to carry me through even the most aggravating weeks.

MY EXPERIENCE WITH ISRAEL'S IAFC

As my work with the children's hospital demonstrates, I am passionate in my support of Israel and have worked to support them in many ways. One particularly meaningful contribution came through about five years of work on the board of the Israeli Air Force Center Foundation (IAFC), located in Herzliya, Israel.

The organization's goal is simple, yet profound: never forget the fallen pilots of Israel, the brave servicemen killed either in action or in training. Given Israel's unique challenges in defending their territories, their Air Force has been instrumental in sustaining the country's existence over the past several decades, and their pilots are often treated like rock stars.

From an American perspective, it might be difficult to appreciate the scale and impact of armed conflict on such a small country. Israeli pilots number in the low thousands. Graduation classes usually number only about fifty or sixty people. When one life is lost, the impact is felt deeply, and the IAFC provides support to the children, spouses, and parents of the fallen pilots.

Much of my work there involved community. Especially during my first few years at the IAFC, we would sponsor retreats for families of fallen service members. At these events, we would bring together about two to four hundred people so they could share their stories with each other and grow stronger by being in each other's presence and remembering their loved ones together.

Also during my time with the IAFC, we developed a cadet program for young students. Everyone serves in Israel after they turn eighteen, but not everyone receives the same basic training and mental preparation ahead of their service.

The IAFC's cadet program has trained thousands of kids who have come through the center. Our focus was on values, on treating their enemies fairly, and on doing the right thing—even when the opposition might not.

In this way, we helped the incoming generation understand the kinds of challenges they might face. Further, it helped build solidarity among the different branches of armed service. Not every cadet who came through the IAFC program would end up in the highly competitive Air Force, but they would all have a shared sense of values.

Research is another important part of the IAFC's work. During my time there, the IAFC supported research into unmanned drone ambulances that would fly into a war zone, pick up an injured soldier, and get them to safety. Research shows that wounded combatants are much more likely to survive if they can be treated within the first hour, and these medical drones would be able to reach places where the risk of a manned helicopter mission was too great.

I'm still involved in the IAFC, though I'm no longer a board member. One thing I've learned in my charitable activities is that boards should bring in new blood. Not only does it protect against complacency, but it also reinvigorates the process with new members' enthusiasm.

It's also more practical financially. After all, a board member can only call the same group of people to fundraise so many times. The more you refresh your board, the more newer contacts your charity or nonprofit will develop.

SAM ZISES AND THE IMPORTANCE OF GIVING

My friend and business leader Sam Zises considers charity a very personal subject—and a very nuanced one. While charitable acts might not be entirely selfless, Sam doesn't see them as selfish either. This might be why everybody has a different idea of giving back.

"There are companies that build this concept directly into their model, be it the Tom's Shoes or the Warby Parkers of the world," Sam says. "Then, there are others that simply make it a priority to invest some of their profits into local or personally important causes."

Whatever the case, Sam agrees that helping your community or others around the world contributes to the goodness of society. "If you've had success in your life or have been fortunate enough to have access to more than you need, giving back and operating with a charitable heart will only warm you inside," Sam says.

Even the more successful among us may one day depend on the kindness of others. We each face our own challenges, and in Sam's case it meant putting his own charitable motivations to the test in the process:

> *I don't often love mixing business and personal relationships, but every so often the opportunity presents itself, and for the most part, it has worked out well. My firm recently took on a project a friend hired us for, which happened to be for a high-profile charity, one I respect and that undoubtedly does incredible work. Several months into the project, it became clear expectations were not aligned. What would have turned out to be a breakeven project for my firm became a costly expense. For personal, professional, and charitable reasons, we did our best and finished the project. Sometimes in life you have to pick your battles. Knowing which ones to pick can be a lot easier when you've got a sense of what's right.*

Having learned plenty of his own lessons, Sam believes the most important lesson for aspiring leaders is finding a mentor you admire. "More important than surrounding yourself with associates you like and respect is ensuring you put yourself in a position to learn from and work closely with a boss you admire, someone who can become a mentor, knowingly or not."

In the business world, Sam says, "There is no substitute for experience, and becoming an expert requires just that." When it comes to experience, there are no short-cuts. "The only way to get it is to go through it," he says, and having a mentor you can respect and learn from will only help the process.

Sam says the most important lesson he has learned as a leader is empathy. "Every good relationship requires a level of empathy for one another," he says. "Running any business requires collaboration—which is all about relationships." No matter the industry, leaders must interact daily with vendors, clients, and employees, just to name a few. If you can't understand where they're coming from, you're going to have a rough time.

Plenty of leadership books offer advice on problem-solving, keeping overhead low, and leading with conviction. However, Sam says, "Few business books or resources I have read have gone deep into the requirements a leader must have in being able to empathize with those around them."

This isn't always easy. "As the leader of the pack with the most at stake, it'd be nice to feel like those around you have empathy for you, but life doesn't always work that way," Sam says. In other words, if you want empathy from others, you must be prepared to show it.

Poise and composure are key parts of leadership, but so is understanding others' needs. "As leaders," Sam says, "we are the ones who must keep the trains running on time—no matter what. Having empathy means understanding when an employee has to leave the office in the middle of the week to 'deal with personal issues.'"

In those situations, Sam's advice is simple: be supportive. "Show compassion when a vendor misses a delivery because they've been pressed for time. Having empathy is at the heart of keeping relationships successful, and great relationships are integral to being a great leader."

EXERCISE: WHAT ROLE DOES CHARITY PLAY IN YOUR LIFE?

Being a good business leader isn't just about closing the most deals and earning the best living. It's not about being perfect. It's about being a complete person. In my experience, a big part of becoming that person is being generous to your community and working to strengthen your bonds with others. Use the space below to answer the following questions.

1. Do you conduct yourself with a charitable heart?

2. What are some ways you can give back to your community?

3. How can you incorporate a charitable mindset into your leadership role?

4. How does charity impact you in everyday life?

DO YOUR BEST—AND BE GRATEFUL

I've continuously stressed to my children that I'm not perfect. I try to do the best I can, but I make mistakes like anyone else. I stress this because I see it as part of setting a good example. Get involved, work hard, contribute to your community, but above all, do the right thing—even if that means admitting when you're wrong.

Business is no different. Just as you can choose to be an ethical parent, you can choose to be an ethical business leader rather than someone who cuts corners or uses cutthroat strategies.

You set the example. Whether you choose to give time and resources to your community or you choose to cheat and undermine others around you, don't be surprised when you see your children or employees acting the same way.

This isn't to say we're doomed to become our parents or our bosses. We can always bend the trajectory and choose to do the right thing. In that same way, we can choose to model better behaviors for those who look up to us and to take control of the example we're setting.

I value charitable activities, because I see it as a way of showing gratitude for my community. I was fortunate to have parents, especially my mother, who constantly modeled this for me.

My early life is filled with countless examples of my mother's charity, of all the ways she found to show her appreciation for life and the people she shared her life with.

For instance, when my parents sold their house, they realized many of their prized possessions couldn't come with them. It would have been easy for them to throw a tag sale and make some money off these items, but my mother had a better idea. Instead of the sale, she invited all her employees over to take something as a token of her gratitude for all they had given her.

Later, when she was diagnosed with cancer and given only a few months to live, this same gratitude for life sustained her through countless rounds of chemotherapy and other treatments. She appreciated everybody's help, but she would take none of their sympathy. "Oh, everyone has cancer. Everybody's gotta die of something," she would say in her characteristic sense of humor. "I'm planning on living, and I'm going to live, okay?"

I like to think the life she had given so much to was giving itself back to her in her final years. Three months stretched to a year, which ultimately stretched to five before the cancer finally took her.

When she passed, we cried tears of pride and joy, not sadness. We knew she had milked life to its last day, and when the time came, she went gracefully. Even in death, she set examples for me to follow.

Whether you're acting as a parent or a business leader, you have the ability to set the message about how you contend with adversity, how you deal with success, and how you treat your community.

You don't have to be perfect. You can make mistakes. If you set a good example, however, you will forever have people to support you and lift you up when you need them.

Conclusion

· · · · ·

From my earliest memories, I knew my brothers and I were blessed to have parents who were honorable, had a great work ethic, built us up, and encouraged us to be great people as well. I pray that I have done the same for my children, and that I can continue to do so now that they're grown and finding their own success.

Even more, I hope everyone else I've mentored over the years can take the lessons I've shared with them, make them their own, and then share them with others—their coworkers, their spouses, their children, and the rest of their community.

If you take away one concept from this book, one thing you admire about my family's approach to leadership, one story or motto that offers you a guiding light, then I have been successful.

As we wrap up our time together, I want to take you back to the beginning of our first chapter, back to Sam Darnold's star-making turn in that fateful game between Penn State and USC. However old you are, whether you're a student yourself or an experienced professional moving forward with your career, I hope you can relate to Darnold's example and understand what strong leadership looks like.

I hope you can relate to someone who took the most positive aspects of his personality—discipline, training, thinking things through, a positive attitude, and more than a little heart and soul—and put them all on display on a national stage as he led his team to victory.

Now ask yourself: how do you become that kind of person?

Through this book, I've given you the ingredients. However, it's up to you to perfect the recipe.

The lucky part is this isn't the Rose Bowl. Most of us don't have to live with the game on the line before it's over and the world moves on. We have a much longer window for making things happen and becoming truly great at what we do.

However, like Sam Darnold, we have a responsibility to make every minute count, as sometimes that extra bit of fire you bring in that last moment will make all the difference.

Always remember that no matter what happens today, tomorrow you have another chance. Each day, you get to start over and see if you can do better than the day before.

No matter where the next day takes you, remember to do the right thing.

KEEP IN TOUCH

Just as I've shared with you, I hope you'll share what you've learned with others.

Even more, I hope you'll share with me.

Visit my blog and leave a comment: https://glennedwards. wordpress.com.

Or e-mail me: gedwards@chartorg.com.

Suggestions for Further Reading

· · · · ·

Ready to keep learning? Here are some books that have influenced me along the way.

Atlas Shrugged and *The Fountainhead*, by Ayn Rand. These two novels have helped shape my ideas of fairness in business and government, specifically in the artificial ways subsidies are used to prop up struggling industries. Essentially, if something can't make money on its own, then people shouldn't be compelled to support it.

Crime and Punishment, by Fyodor Dostoyevsky. As with Ayn Rand's books, many of the messages I read here directly shaped my adult life. The idea here is if you do something wrong, even if you get away with it, that doesn't make it right. I've found this a common theme in life and think it's an incredibly important lesson for young people to learn.

MBA: Management by Auerbach, by Red Auerbach. Here, the famed former NBA coach explores the many similarities between planning and strategizing in both basketball and business. Some of my favorite tips: make sure you have people who complement each other, know what your competition is doing, and put out a great product every day.

Start-Up Nation: The Story of Israel's Economic Miracle, by Dan Senor and Saul Singer. The modern Israel hasn't been a nation for very long, and yet in that time, the country has seen tremendous growth and innovation, contributing greatly to areas like tech and agriculture. This feat is all the more impressive for such a small nation in such a hostile environment.

The Tipping Point, by Malcolm Gladwell. Whether in business or in life, everything we do reaches a point where it either collapses under its own weight or, more ideally, propels you to new levels of success. I like this book because it shows you how this works and what to look for in your own life to make sure things tip in your favor.

Two Turns from Zero, by Stacey Griffith. You don't have to be a fitness enthusiast for this book to inspire you. What I like about this book is its overwhelmingly positive and supportive message and the way Griffith takes what she's learned from a lifetime of teaching spinning classes and transformed them into essential life lessons.

About the Author

· · · · ·

GLENN EDWARDS joined his parents' family business in 1980 after graduating from Stony Brook University. After growing the company to become one of the largest home health-care firms on the East Coast, he sold it in 2005. His investment company, Chart Organization, LLC, has holdings in commercial real estate, multifamily residential, retail stores, and recreation companies.

Today, Glenn serves alongside his children, Jordan and Gabrielle, at Mixology, a fashion retailer founded by his longtime friends and partners, the Shapiro family. A firm believer in building strong communities, Glenn has served on the boards of numerous charitable organizations throughout his career.

www.ingramcontent.com/pod-product-compliance
Lightning Source LLC
Chambersburg PA
CBHW071548200326

41519CB00021BB/6660